Making The Jump:

How To Land Your Dream Job When You Get Out Of College

"Practical, proven techniques that will both help you to find the job that you want and make it yours!"

Dr. Jim Anderson

Copyright © 2012 by Dr. Jim Anderson

All rights reserved. No part of this book may be reproduced of transmitted in any form or by any means, electronic or mechanical, including photocopying, recording or by any information storage and retrieval system without written permission of the publisher, except for inclusion of brief quotations in a review.

Printed in the United States of America

Library of Congress Control Number: 2012915149
ISBN-13: 978-1480051287
ISBN-10: 1480051284

Warning – Disclaimer

The purpose of this book is to educate and entertain. This book does not promise or guarantee that anyone following the ideas, tips, suggestions, techniques or strategies will be hired. It is the discretion of employers if you will or will not be hired. The author, publisher and distributor(s) shall have neither liability nor responsibility to anyone with respect to any loss or damage caused, or alleged to be caused, directly or indirectly by the information contained in this book.

Acknowledgements

Any book like this one is the result of years of real-world work experience. In my over 25 years of working for 6 different firms, I have met countless fantastic people and I've been mentored by some truly exceptional ones. Although I've probably forgotten some of the people who made me the person that I am today, here is my attempt to finally give them the recognition that they so truly deserve:

- Thomas P. Anderson
- Art Puett
- Bobbi Marschall
- Bob Boggs
- Chandan Sharma

Dr. Jim Anderson

This book is dedicated to my wife Lori. None of this would have been possible without her love and support.

Thanks for the best 21 years of my life (so far)...!

Table Of Contents

WHAT'S THE BEST WAY TO START? VIII

ABOUT THE AUTHOR...X

CHAPTER 1: GETTING READY FOR THE REAL WORLD 2

CHAPTER 2: MY STORY 14

CHAPTER 3: HOW TO GET WORK EXPERIENCE – BEFORE YOU LEAVE SCHOOL...20

CHAPTER 4: HOW TO PICK THE RIGHT JOB FOR YOU 27

CHAPTER 5: HOW TO USE LINKEDIN TO FIND A JOB 35

CHAPTER 6: HOW TO CREATE A RESUME THAT WILL GET YOU THE INTERVIEW..58

CHAPTER 7: HOW TO WRITE A COVER LETTER / EMAIL THAT WILL GET YOUR RESUME READ 76

CHAPTER 8: HOW TO MASTER THE INTERVIEW PROCESS 84

CHAPTER 9: HOW TO STAND OUT FROM EVERYONE ELSE WHO IS LOOKING FOR THE JOB THAT YOU WANT 109

CHAPTER 10: HOW TO FOLLOW UP THE INTERVIEW SO THAT YOU'LL BE REMEMBERED 116

CHAPTER 11: PERSISTENCE, PERSISTENCE, PERSISTENCE 126

CHAPTER 12: THE VIEW FROM THE OTHER SIDE: WHAT EMPLOYERS ARE LOOKING FOR..130

APPENDIX A: GOALS FOR YOUR JOB SEARCH................................140

APPENDIX B: WHAT YOU NEED TO LEARN FROM EVERY COLLEGE JOB 143

APPENDIX C: WHAT TO DO AFTER YOU GET THE PERFECT JOB 145

APPENDIX D: 100 COMMON INTERVIEW QUESTIONS....................147

APPENDIX E: GOOD QUESTIONS FOR YOU TO ASK DURING AN INTERVIEW..154

Table Of Figures

FIGURE 1: EXAMPLE OF SOME OF THE OVER 1M GROUPS IN LINKEDIN 40
FIGURE 2: MANY "HIDDEN" JOBS MAY BE POSTED ON A GROUP'S JOBS TAB 41
FIGURE 3: JOBS MAY BE LISTED AS A PART OF A COMPANY'S LINKEDIN PAGE..........42
FIGURE 4: HOW TO POST AN UPDATE TO YOUR LINKEDIN PROFILE........................44
FIGURE 5: BE SURE TO KEEP NOTES ON EACH OF YOUR LINKEDIN CONTACTS..........45
FIGURE 6: LINKEDIN WILL SHOW YOU JOBS BASED ON YOUR PROFILE 49
FIGURE 7: YOU CAN ANSWER QUESTIONS ASKED BY OTHER LINKEDIN USERS..........52
FIGURE 8: LINKEDIN ALLOWS YOU TO "FOLLOW" COMPANIES THAT INTEREST YOU .54
FIGURE 9: LINKEDIN'S LIST OF EVENTS ALLOWS YOU TO MEET REAL PEOPLE 56
FIGURE 10: EXAMPLE OF A RESUME HEADER 64
FIGURE 11: SAMPLE STRENGTHS SECTION OF A RESUME....................................67
FIGURE 12: SAMPLE EDUCATION SECTION OF A RESUME 68
FIGURE 13: SAMPLE EDUCATION SECTION OF A RESUME BEFORE GRADUATION 68
FIGURE 14: SAMPLE EDUCATION SECTION WITH MULTIPLE DEGREES 68
FIGURE 15: SAMPLE EXPERIENCE DESCRIPTION..69
FIGURE 16: SAMPLE COMPLETE RESUME...74

What's The Best Way To Start?

Going to college is a fantastic time in your life. Yes, yes – I realize that it may not always seem that way what with all of those tests, your parents hounding you about last semester's grades, relationships that were so strong but suddenly went away and various physical maladies that may afflict you. Take it from an old guy (me), you'll eventually look back on your college days and will only be able to remember the good stuff.

The problem with college is that once you finally get good at it, after 4, 5, or even 6 years in college, it's all over. You've screwed up big time and now you're looking at graduating. What then? Sure, you could go to graduate school and put off the inevitable for a while longer, but it's going to happen someday – you'll have to leave college and enter into that scary place that we call "the real world".

It turns out that this transition from working to get a college degree to starting to use that college degree as part of your first professional job can be made to be a lot less scary. What you need to do is to understand that it's going to happen and then start to prepare for it.

I'm hoping that you are reading these words as somebody who is just preparing to enter into college. However, if you are like me, there is a good chance that you've put off the whole "how am I going to find my first job" thing until (much) later in the game. No matter, if you are a freshman, sophomore, junior or even a senior in college, this book will show you step-by-step what you are going to have to do in order to identify the job that you want and then how to go out and get it.

I am the proud owner of four different college degrees. Each degree was earned by planting my butt in a chair and sitting through countless classes, taking far too many tests, and turning in mountains of homework. Believe me when I say, "I feel your pain."

It turns out that this finding of a first job after you graduate from college is not all that hard to do. Look at it this way, people have been graduating from college forever and each year thousands of new graduates stream out of colleges all across the country and they all seem to somehow end up working at a job in a fairly short period of time. Sure there are always some exceptions, but we're talking about most people here.

This means that you've got some pretty good odds that you are going to find a job after you graduate. However, I want you to do just a little bit better than that: I want you to find the perfect job for you. Make sure that you check out Appendix A for a list of the goals that you'll want to accomplish on your way to getting the perfect first job for you.

You can jump into this book anywhere. I've written each chapter for both the person who started looking for their first job as a freshman and for everyone else. This means that there's something for you in each chapter. I'd ask that you at least leaf through the first few chapters just to make sure that you know what you should be looking for.

Good luck!

- Dr. Jim Anderson, September 2012

About The Author

College has been a part of my life from the very beginning. My dad, Tom Anderson, became a full professor at a very young age and over the course of his career he taught at Northwestern University, the University of Iowa, and Southern Illinois University at Edwardsville. Needless to say, I grew up in a number of different college towns.

My college adventure started when I left high school half way through my Senior year and started attending the local university. Sure I had finished all of my required courses, but come on Mom & Dad, it was my Senior year!

My undergraduate adventure was split between attending Southern Illinois University at Edwardsville for the first two years and then attending Washington University in St. Louis for the next two years, after which I graduated.

I'd like to say that I followed all of the suggestions in this book in order to land my first job. The truth is that I probably only did about half of them – simply because there was nobody to tell me what I needed to do! I'm also willing to admit, that in my case, a bit of luck did play a role.

One important point that I have to confess to is that I didn't start even thinking about finding a job until about half way through my Junior year when some of my friends who were Seniors started their own job search. It was sort of like, "Oh wow, you mean that we have to find jobs – they won't come looking for us?" I'd like to think that I'm smarter now than I was back then.

It turns out that I was very good at going to college – I understood how to do it! Once I got out into the real world, I kept going back to college over and over again. I ended up with a collection of four different college degrees: BS, MS, and PhD in Computer Science and an MBA in Marketing. Now I have three children and Mrs. Anderson won't let me go to school any more.

I've spent over 25 years working in the so-called "real world". During that time I've had the opportunity to do my fair share of interviewing and selecting of new college grads. Trust me when I tell you that I have first-hand knowledge of what it takes to be the job candidate that gets selected for a position.

I now live in Tampa Florida where I spend my time managing my consulting business, Blue Elephant Consulting, teaching college courses at the University of South Florida, and traveling to college campus like yours to share the knowledge that I have about how college students can prepare for and get the job that they really want when they finally make the jump to the real world.

I'm always available to answer questions and I can be reached at:

Dr. Jim Anderson
Blue Elephant Consulting
Email: jim@BlueElephantConsulting.com
Facebook: http://goo.gl/1TVoK
Web: http://www.BlueElephantConsulting.com/

"Unforgettable communication skills that will set your ideas free..."

America's Top Student Career Speaker!

Dr. Jim Anderson is available to present his speeches to college student audiences nationwide.

Dr. Anderson believes that in order to both learn and remember what he says, students need to laugh. Each one of his speeches is full of fun and humor so that what he says "sticks" with everyone.

Dr. Anderson's Speech Topics:

- **How To Find The Right 1st Job Using LinkedIn**
    - How to find companies who have the jobs that you'll want.
- **10 Secrets For Having A Great Career**
    - How to get recognized for the work that you do.
- **How To Create & Give Fantastic Presentations**
    - How to connect the opening to the closing
- **Ethics Are Sooo Boring... Until You're Going To Jail!**
    - How to recognize an ethical problem.

Dr. Jim Anderson presents over 100 speeches per year. To invite Dr. Anderson to speak at your event, contact him at:

Phone: 813-418-6970 or
Email: jim@BlueElephantConsulting.com

Chapter 1

Getting Ready For The Real World

Chapter 1:
Getting Ready For The Real World

Congratulations – you went to college! No matter what else happens in your life, you are going to be able to point to the college degree that you're going to get and say "I did this!" Attending college and graduating with a degree is a very big deal – you will have shown the world that you can make a decision, work to accomplish a goal, and keep at it for several years until you achieve it. You'd be amazed at the number of people who can't do what you are doing right now.

If this was all that it took to land the perfect job, then there would be no need for this book. However, it's not and that's why this book exists. Just getting a college degree does not (1) guarantee you a job or (2) guarantee you the perfect job for you. Both of these things start with you getting your degree, but from there it's going to take some effort on your part to make it happen.

The good news is that the perfect job for you is out there. Unfortunately, it's not clear just exactly where it is. Additionally, it's not going to just come walking up to you and present itself. Instead, you're going to have to do some research and some planning in order to be able to land the job that you really want once you're out of college.

All too often when I talk with recent college graduates, they are depressed about their prospects for finding any job let alone the perfect job for them. Perhaps they got a late start on the job hunt or maybe they've been going about it all wrong. No matter, what both they and you need to realize is that the world has a desperate need for you and your skills. There is a job out there waiting for you. All that you have to do is to find it and convince the people who are in charge that you are the perfect fit for that job.

How to make this happen is exactly what this book is all about. We're going to start at the beginning and we'll take you through the entire process. We're going to be covering everything that you need to know about how to find the right job for you and then how to make sure that the people who are doing the hiring see you as the perfect candidate for that job.

One important thing that you are going to have to do is to treat your job hunt as what it really is – a job. No matter where you are in school, guess what, you've now got a job. No, you probably won't be spending 40 hours per week working at this job (nor should you). However, you will need to show some tenacity and do a little bit of work all the time throughout your time in college. Oh, in case you were wondering – you don't get paid for this job. Instead, you'll end up with the perfect job. Now that's not a bad trade, is it?

What is the right job for you?

Before we waste any time talking about how you can find and land the perfect job for you, let's take just a moment and spend some time thinking about what your perfect job looks like. The worst thing that we could do would be to successfully get you the wrong job!

There are all sorts of career assessment quizzes that you can take (see your campus career center for help with this). However, in my experience it all boils down to how you answer three critical questions:

1. **Do you like to work with people or do you want to work by yourself?**
   This is a critical one – there is no wrong answer here. Some of us just want to hunker down and do our work and be left alone. Others desperately need human interaction in order to feel complete. Either answer is correct – just make sure that you know which one you prefer so that you don't end up picking a job that requires you to spend a lot of time doing the other thing.

2. **Do you want to collect, process, or format data?**
   I'd like to be able to tell you that your first job out of college will put you into a senior management position, but that wouldn't be true. It's much more likely that you are going to end up doing one of three different types of tasks for the company. First, you may be collecting data for the company. Next, you may be processing that data to transform it into something else. Finally, you may be taking that transformed data and formatting it to be shared with others. Each one of these types of tasks calls for a different set of skills. Which one holds the most interest for you?

3. **Do you want to work in an office or in the field?**
   Once again, this is a big one. Here in the 21st Century the concept of going into an office and working in a cube all day still exists, but there are alternatives. You need to take a moment and picture yourself in an office environment or at a customer site or staring out the windshield of your car as you drive to a new location. Which one of these scenarios fills you with dread?

Which ones could you live with? The decision is a personal one, but knowing the answer BEFORE you go hunting for a job is critical.

3 Skills You'll Need For A Successful Job Hunt

Above and beyond the skills that you are going to need in order to have a successful career while working at whatever job you eventually end up choosing, you're going to need 3 more skills just to be able to get the job that you want.

Your job hunt is going to take some time. Yes, some people get lucky and a job falls into their lap right off the bat. Let's assume that you are not one of those people and it's going to take you the regular amount of time (6 – 12 months) to find your first professional job.

What this means for you is that you are going to have to be able to start your job hunt and then keep at it. Although this may be easy to say, it can be quite difficult to actually do. That's where the following 3 important facts come into play.

Fact #1: There will be setbacks, get over it

Your first job search and every one that comes after it will all share a similar characteristic – they can be a bit frustrating. I mean, you find the job that you want, you go apply for it, and you get it. That's all there is to it. Right? Well, no – not exactly.

You'll find jobs that you think that you are a perfect fit for and they'll go to somebody else. You'll have classmates whom you know are not nearly as smart / talented / gifted as you are get jobs right off the bat while you are still on the hunt with no real prospects in sight. You might even encounter a situation where a company offers you a job and then has to tell you that things have changed and they no longer have a job to offer to you.

How are you going to handle these setbacks? It can be all too easy to throw your hands up and say "I give up" after a few things just don't go your way. I know that you won't stop your job hunt because of such things, but you might be tempted to just take any old job that comes along after a few setbacks.

Don't. I realize that this is both the natural and the easy way to go, but it's also the wrong route for you to take. "Man up" as they like to say and roll with the punches when they come your way. In the end you will be successful and you will be able to get the perfect job for you. However, this is only going to happen if you are able to stay the course and not give up just because you've experienced a few setbacks.

Fact #2: A job hunt is a journey, plan for it...

We all know what you want to accomplish with your job hunt: landing the perfect job for you. However, that's not going to happen overnight. In order to make it happen, a number of things are going to have to happen first.

Instead of completely focusing on the final result (getting the perfect job), you need to identify a set of interim goals that are going to lead you to your final result. These goals will serve you in two ways. First, they'll take a big task (finding you the perfect job) and break it up into a set of smaller, more manageable tasks. Secondly, since the job hunt is a journey, it's all too easy to lose your way and to become disheartened along the way. Having a set of goals that you can check off as you accomplish them will help to keep you both motivated and on track.

Fact #3: You're Good Enough; You're Smart Enough, and Doggone It, People Like You!

You are going to do this. You are going to find the perfect job for you. It may take a while, in fact it may take longer than you want it to, but in the end you will be successful. During your hunt, you need to believe in yourself.

I'd like to be able to tell you that the world is going to be there to support you during your hunt. However, all too often it seems that the opposite is true: you'll be getting negative signals from everyone that you encounter. People will tell you that you don't have the skills that they are looking for, perhaps they are looking for someone with a higher GPA, or maybe they just think that you are too young or too immature for the job that they are trying to fill. Keep in mind that they can believe anything that they want, you know just how good and talented you are. You know that you're going to do great at whatever job you finally get and everyone else really doesn't matter.

When all of those roadblocks show up during your job hunt, you need to learn to look beyond them. Yes, they are an immediate problem, but realize that they will soon be forgotten as you move on and get that much closer to your final goal of landing the perfect job for you.

What It All Means

This is going to be your job hunt. You own it all – the obstacles, the challenges, and the final successful results. I can tell you that if you keep at it long enough, you will eventually be successful. However, the one thing that I can't tell you is how long the journey is going to be.

As long as you are able to deal with the setbacks that you will encounter, create goals that will see you through to the end of your job hunt, and keep believing in yourself, then you are going to be successful. I believe in you, now you have to do the same!

Your Job Hunt Time Line

In all honesty, your job hunt should take you 4 years. If you are a sophomore, junior, or even a senior don't despair! In this book we've got you covered and we can speed up the process for you.

However, for just a moment let's talk about the ideal case: what should an incoming freshman do starting in year one in order to be ready to go out and land the perfect job four years later? It turns out that it's actually pretty simple…

Freshman Year

1. **Get a clue:** Let's face it, when we show up as freshman we really don't have a clue as to what we want to do with our lives. Freshman year is a great time to sort this out. Find out where your college's career services office is and go check out the material that they have on various careers and majors. Just because you picked a major already does not mean that you have to stick with it. Let the smart career counselors help you to find out what interests, skills, and preferences you have, and generally what's important to you.

2. **Start to build your network:** From your professors to the folks who work at the university's career center, you need to spend time making some new friends. You want these people to agree to be part of your extended

network. They'll be able to help you out when it comes time to ask for referrals or to discuss specific job or internship related questions and concerns.

3. **Get a job:** Well, not a real job but rather check out the possibility of landing one of the available internship or co-op opportunities and to get advice about applying for and obtaining these positions from the folks at the career center. You might not land one your freshman year, but at least you'll learn how the system works and you'll boost your odds of being successful next year.

Sophomore Year

1. **Get Involved:** You don't want to be a peon your entire career, you'd like to rise into the senior ranks. Show your future employer that you have the right stuff by getting involved in on campus organizations and taking on leadership roles in them.

2. **Narrow Your Career List**: Pick a few careers and majors that you've researched and dive in and go talk to people at the university who work in these areas. This is the time to conduct informational interviews to learn about job fields. Who better to ask than someone who's already doing the job that you think that you might like to do?

3. **Get A Job:** Once again, no matter how appealing a job may SOUND, you won't really know if it's right for you until you do it or something close to it. Take the time to apply for part-time, seasonal, or internship positions in your area of interest to actually "try on" a career before

making a commitment to it. It's sort of like getting a temporary tattoo before getting real ink.

Junior Year

1. **Pick A Major**: Sorry about this, it's time to pull the trigger and finally decide what you want to be when you grow up. With a little luck you've thought about different careers and this is the area that you kept coming back to. This IS like getting a tattoo – it's permanent and everyone is going to be able to see it.

2. **Get Serious About Getting A Job**: This is the time to knuckle down and get an internship or a co-op job. This experience is going to go a long way in helping you to prepare your application materials and will help you to begin building work experience that will make a difference come graduation time.

3. **Get Career Involved**: Take part in on-campus group organizations that relate to your major. Student branches of professional organizations (such as the IEEE, ASME, AMA, or the ABA) are great choices. These activities will be easily recognized on your resume during an interview

Senior Year

1. **Build Your Job Search:** Now is the time to be packaging your college expertise, work and internship experience, and leadership qualities that you've been developing while in school. The goal is to use all of this information

to focus your job search on those firms that you believe will have the perfect job for you.

2. **Start Your Job Search:** It's time to go back to the career center and ask for help in starting your job search. This may include creating an effective job search strategy using a variety of different tools: on-campus recruiting, job fairs, targeted approaches to desired employers, networking with professionals in your field, smart use of online resources, etc.

3. **Get Some Help:** Your campus career center exists for one reason – to help you get a job. Use them! Take advantage of all of the services that they offer during the year and don't wait until the end of the year to work with them because that's exactly when everyone else is going to be doing the same thing!

The One Thing That You Have To Sell: Yourself!

If I can leave you with one final thought from this chapter, then let it be this; you are selling a product to any firm that you are interested in going to work for. You are the product.

What this means is that during your job hunt, you are officially a member of the sales department. What this means is that how you present the product (you) is going to be very important in determining if you are able to make a sale. People do form first impressions that are very hard to shake.

I'm sorry to say it, but this means that all of those piercings that you have must disappear during the job search process. Any tattoos that you decided were something that you just HAD to have need to be covered up and you've got to be on your best behavior.

Think of yourself as an actor and you're playing the role of a job seeker. You want this story to have a happy ending! There are a lot of other people out there trying to get the company to "buy" them to fill the job that you want. You need to do a better job of selling than they do.

I hope that you don't feel too overwhelmed. Lots of people have done this before you and you will be successful. I'm going to show you what you need to do in order to prepare, create a plan, and follow through. We're going to get you the perfect job!

Chapter 2

My College Story

Chapter 2: My Story

When I graduated from high school, I had no idea what I wanted to do with my life. Pretty much the only thing that I did know was that I was going to go to college. I wish that I could tell you that I was committed to going to college for all the right reasons: a desire to continue my education, an understanding that a college degree is the ticket to a successful career, etc.

However, the real reason that I went to college is probably pretty much the same reason that you went to college – it was what everyone else was doing and my parents expected me to do it. Enough said.

My Time In College

My college career was split between two very different schools. I started out by attending Southern Illinois University at Edwardsville. It was in my home town, easy to get into, and my dad taught there – a no brainer.

I went to SIUE for two years and it turns out that it was a good thing that I did. I had no idea what I had gotten myself into. My independent study skills were not very good and I struggled initially trying to focus enough to get all of that freshman weed-out work done.

Somehow I limped through my first two years with a decent GPA. My parents suggested that it was time for me to "go off to college" (were they trying to get rid of me?) and so I started applying to different schools.

In my case, I applied to what seemed like a million colleges (that fancy Common Application thing didn't exist back in the day) and I was soundly rejected by just about all of them. Guess who had not spent his high school years getting ready for college? I finally weaseled my way into a school and I was off and running.

My final two years of undergraduate college were spent at Washington University in St. Louis. I had a great time there! My grades pretty much reflected the fact that I had a great time there, but somehow I was able to keep it together enough to academically limp through my junior and senior years.

Working While In College

I worked during my first two years of college because I had the time. I didn't work during my last two years because I was overwhelmed with work. When I was working, I got lucky and the only jobs that were available just happened to be in my major area.

I had selected Computer Science for my major primarily because I happened to be very good at the video game Asteroids. Sorry – you were thinking that there had to be a better reason for choosing one's life purpose?

My first job was working as a lab assistant at a computer lab that was a part of the university's school of education. This turned out to be a great job because I got to help education majors (mostly girls) solve very basic computer problems and I came across looking like a very smart guy. Not too bad for a nerd.

Later on, I was able to get a job working as a computer operator for the Mid-Illinois Computer Cooperative (MICC). Basically, I spent my time changing magnetic tapes on a mainframe computer. Oh, and playing a crude form of Asteroids on the operator console. Best job ever!

While working at both of these jobs, I had a very important realization: there were jobs that related to computers that I didn't like to do. It turns out that any work experience that you can get during your college career will end up teaching you two things.

The first is what you like to do. Hopefully, some part of the tasks that you are asked to do will appeal to you – working with people, solving problems, making presentations, etc. What too many college students don't realize is that at the same time you are going to be learning what you don't like to do.

It may turn out that you don't like to work with people. Perhaps you don't like to sit in a cube for 8-10 hours every day. There can be a number of different things that turn you off. This is the time to find out what they are.

In Appendix B in this book, I've included a worksheet that will help you to capture the things that each job that you have will teach you. Use it so that when it comes time to build your job search you can refer to it and make sure that you only go looking for jobs that are going to make you happy.

Getting The Perfect Job (For Me)

Like most college students, I changed my major. In my case I waited until half way through my junior year before I did it, and then only because the major that I had been working on was turning out to be too hard and so I picked something easier.

Once I had done this, it was time for me to get serious about starting to look for a job. I was smart enough to know that I had no clue about how to interview for a job and so at the end of my junior year I signed up for some job interviews. Somehow I forgot to mention to anyone that I was only a junior and wouldn't be graduating for another year.

As you can well imagine, those interviews were the worst ones that I've ever done. I hadn't prepared, I didn't know answers to some pretty basic questions, and I was so nervous that I stumbled over all of my answers.

As poorly as I did, the learning experience, as the folks at MasterCard would say, was priceless. By the last interview of the year, I had gotten my act together and could actually do a passable job.

Over the summer a friend of mine who was really getting ready to graduate was going to a local job fair and he asked me to come along for moral support. I grabbed a couple copies of my resume and tagged along. I dropped off copies of my resume everywhere I could find someone who would take it. I didn't think about the job fair again.

It was roughly half way through my senior year that I got a call from the McDonnell Douglas Aircraft Company. They said that they had gotten a copy of my resume from the job fair and would I like to come in for an interview. Would I!

My interviewing practice the year before, my on campus work experience, and the fact that I had worked out how I wanted to answer the questions that they were asking all resulted in one of the best job interviews I've ever had during my career. I got the job!

My Success Means That You Are Going To Be Successful

Please listen to me very carefully: if I can do this getting a first job thing, then you can. I fully believe that you've got more going for you than I ever did. You are brighter, smarter, and probably have it much more together than I ever did and so YES – you're going to find a job. Now we just need to make sure that the job that you find is the perfect job for you.

Please note that in my job hunt there was no Harry Potter magic involved. Everything was done the old fashioned way (and since this was all done before cell phones and laptops, it was really old fashioned). Considering all of the 21st Century tools that you now have available to you, there's no way that you can't be successful.

I really don't have a lot of personal skills – I can't sing, I can't dance. However, the one thing that I do have going for me is that I am tenacious. Once I start something, I won't give up until it's done. I need you to become just as tenacious as I am when it comes to your job hunt. Fix your eyes on what you want to achieve and then don't let anything, I do mean anything, keep you from achieving what you know that you can do.

Chapter 3

How To Get Work Experience – Before You Leave School

Chapter 3:
How To Get Work Experience – Before You Leave School

When you are sitting in that interview, wouldn't you like to be able to look the other person in the eye and tell them that you've done the job that you are interviewing for before? That's where getting some work experience while you are in college can really help you out.

When you are going to school, your number one job is to study and pass your classes. This work thing, although important, can get in your way if you aren't careful. That's why you need to come up with a plan for how you are going to combine getting some work experience with completing your college degree. Hmm, looks like you've got a real challenge here!

From the moment that you start your college education to the moment that you walk off that stage with your diploma in your hand, you will have four different ways to gain the work experience that can help you to get your first job.

Not all of these different ways to get work experience will be right for everybody, but at least one of them should work with your schedule and what you want to accomplish while you are in college. Let's take a detailed look at what your options are.

Option #1: Work On Campus

This is an option that just about any student can take advantage of. The trick is going to be what type of job you get.

Every university has an immense need for student workers. There are janitorial positions, clerical positions, teaching assistant positions and lab technician positions. Some of these are going to be right for you and some are not.

During your freshman year, any job will do just fine. What you are going to be trying to do during this year is to build up an on-campus reputation for being reliable and efficient. Your boss for this job will be the person who will serve as a reference when you go for your next on-campus job.

During your sophomore and junior years, you are going to want to look around on campus and identify what kind of work the professors who are teaching the classes in your major are doing. Do they run a lab? Are they out in the field conducting experiments and collecting data?

You are going to want to approach one of your professors and ask them for a job. Getting this job is going to be critical – it's going to show up on your resume as work that you've done that relates to the jobs that you'll be interviewing for.

I almost hate to bring this up, but it really doesn't matter how much you are going to be paid to do this work. The work experience and, with a little luck, getting your professor to agree to be a reference for you are going to be worth their weight in gold.

Option #2: Get A Summer Job

During a standard 4-year college education, you are going to have 3 summer vacations. How you choose to spend these vacations may have a significant impact on how long you have to spend looking for your first job.

The summer between your freshman and sophomore school years is your one chance to (almost) kick back and have a good time. You still need to get a job, but exactly what you spend your time doing is less important than it will be going forward. Simply being able to show that you worked during the summer will help to pad out your resume. Just make sure that wherever you work that you pick up some real world skills.

The next summer, the one between your sophomore and junior years in school, needs to be more focused. You are going to want to get a job that will be related to your major in some way.

I almost hate to bring it up again, but the type of job that you get is more important than the amount of pay that you receive. Having a summer job that prepares you to get a great professional job is worth whatever you give up in lost wages.

Finally we come to the summer between your junior and your senior years. This is your last chance to make an impression on your interviewers. It might be worth it to meet with one or more of the professors who teach in your major and ask them if they have a need for help over the summer.

A job that was clearly in line with the type of work that you want to be doing in your first job is a great way to score points during your interviews. What's going to be most important is that you create a list of stories about what you learned on this job. These are the stories that you can share during your interviews and they'll prove that you already know how to do the job that you are interviewing for.

Option #3: Get An Internship

An internship is good work if you can get it! An internship is a program offered by your college or university that will allow you to work in your major's field of study while at the same time receiving academic credit for it. Note that the number of hours that you can get credit for differs from university to university, but is generally limited to 12-15 credits.

Your university is highly motivated to have you look into an internship. By having you go out and work in the real world, the university is able to showcase their best and brightest students and this results in an improved impression of the university in the local community.

There is always the possibility that your college does not have an internship program set up. Don't let this put you off. Instead, seize the opportunity and get in contact with local firms that are active in your field of study. There is a possibility that you can create your own internship program with them.

Once again, how much you get paid really does not matter – you might even consider doing the work for free if it's the right job. What you are looking for is the ability to add the experience to your resume. Additionally, if you do a good job then you just might be able to get your employer to agree to act as a reference for you. Now that would be time well spent!

Option #4: Get A Real Job

This is the ultimate hard-core option – going out and getting a real off-campus job. In addition to going to college, go out and get a job working for a firm that does something that is related to your field of study.

The biggest cost to this approach is that it is going to consume the largest amount of your time. However, the up side is that it will show up on your resume as a significant piece of employment.

You are going to need to keep in mind that while you are in school, your number one goal is to get through school and graduate. The job is a means to an end, not the end itself. That means that you are going to have to become good at balancing the demands on your time.

Living a double life of a student and worker can be tough on anyone. One thing that you might want to give some careful thought to is just exactly when you'd go out and get a job.

I would recommend that you not do this during your freshman or sophomore years. You've got enough going on during those years that any sort of significant job is going to be too much of a distraction and could end up delaying your progress through school.

Did Somebody Say Networking?

Yes, work experience is important; however, there is something even more valuable that any job that you might have during college can provide you with. That is a network of people who want to see you succeed.

Every person that you encounter while you are working, no matter if they are your boss, your coworkers, or even customers, is important. Use this time to make connections and to find out what makes people really tick. Use every lunch as an opportunity to sit with someone new and find out what they do and how they got to where they are.

Anyone can make contact with someone. The trick is to develop and nurture your network. In order to make this happen you need to stay in contact with the people that you meet. That means that you are going to have to remain aware of what is going on in their lives. This takes some effort, but the results will make it all worthwhile.

The combination of work experience and the people that you've met along the way is what is going to equip you to have a successful job hunt. Yes, both of these things do take both time and effort on your part and I realize that you already have a lot going on in your life while you are in college. However, taking the time to work on both of these tasks right now will pay dividends later on that will make it all well worth the effort that you put into it.

Chapter 4

How To Pick the Right Job For You

Chapter 4:
How To Pick the Right Job For You

What job should you apply for?

Dang it, there was never a class that taught you how to do this! When you have your college degree, it sure seems as though it would be handy if all of the job postings that you ran across were color coded in some way: orange = must have a business degree, blue = must have an engineering degree, etc. Unfortunately, this is not how the real world operates.

You're going to have to keep in mind two things while you are engaged in your job hunt: in order for you to land the perfect job two things are going to have to happen. First, the company with the position is going to have to want to hire you and secondly you are going to have to want to be hired by them. Both parts have to be there or there will be no deal.

What this means for you is that you need to do some reading. You need to take a look at the jobs that are being advertised, read the job description and then sit back and answer 3 questions.

The first question is how do you feel about the company that is advertising the job. I've had a number of friends who were very strongly anti-war. That meant that they never wanted to work in the defense industry. If a defense contractor was advertising a position at their firm, then it was a nonstarter for my friends – they wouldn't even consider it. You need to decide if you'd be willing to go to work for the company that is looking to fill the position that is being advertised.

The next question is do you think that you would enjoy doing this job? We could all probably stack boxes for 12 hours a day, but is that why you just spent 4, 5, or 6 years in college? If so, then that was one expensive box-stacking degree you just got. Any job that you consider should involve skills that you just learned as a part of getting your college degree. This knowledge is what makes you special and is why companies will be willing to hire you versus somebody who just walks in off the street.

Finally, the last question that you need to be able to answer is how does this job fit into your career plans? This position is just a job. Your career will consist of a whole series of jobs that will lead you to where you want to get to. Where is that place? Is it being CEO? Is it eventually owning and running your own company? There is no wrong answer when it comes to picking a career goal; however, each job that you have needs to take you one step closer to realizing that goal.

Step #1: Applying For A Job – Time To Do Some Research

That job posting is not going to stay unfilled forever, so you don't have an unlimited amount of time here. You're going to need to use the time that you have to do some research. You're good at that, right? I mean, that's the kind of thing that you do in collage as a part of your classes all the time...

The things that you are going to want to research are the position that the company is trying to fill and the company itself. One way to go about doing this is to talk to others who work in the same field and, even better, who work in the same profession as the job opening. If you don't know anybody who has a job like this, don't worry. We're going to be talking about how to use LinkedIn later on in this book and that's exactly the type of thing that LinkedIn is great at helping you to do.

When you find the right people to talk to, you're going to want to ask them the right questions. These will include asking about the competitive landscape – what are other firms in this area doing? You'll also want to find out about best practices for a job like this. How do people do this kind of work – are there industry standards that need to be followed? What you are trying to do here is to get a good understanding of the company, its open position, and what skills the job is going to require.

Step #2: Applying For A Job – Getting Honest Feedback

So, are you the right person for this job? Who knows? You may want to apply for the job, but should you? The best people to ask are the ones who know you the best.

This is the time to print out the job description that you are interested in and head on out to have some talks. What you want to do is to find people whose opinion you trust and ask them to look at the job description and then tell you if you have what it takes to do the job. You're really going to want to have this talk with more than one person.

You are not looking for a simple "yes" or "no" here. Instead, what you'd like these very special people to do for you is to pinpoint both your strengths and your weaknesses. Your best friend may not be the right person for this job. You desperately need honest feedback – you don't need your Mom telling you that you're the best and any firm would be lucky to have you.

What you should be looking for in their feedback is a list of areas where you could improve. Nobody out there is perfect – including you! If they tell you that they can't think of any area where you could improve, then move on – they were the wrong people to talk to.

This, of course, leads to the big question – just exactly who should you be asking to help evaluate you and the job posting? What I've found is that it often most helpful to find folks who are currently working in senior management positions – almost like the people who will eventually be interviewing you. These people have been out there for a while and have been working long enough to know what works in the real world.

The people that you most want to talk to have had assistance during their careers. They've received guidance from others as they climbed the career ladder at their company. Generally speaking, these people are going to be more advanced in their careers.

The benefit for you from these types of discussions is going to be that they won't hold back: they'll tell you what's what. These people want to help you and so they'll let you know if the job posting that you've shown to them is not right for you. What's even better is that if they don't think that the job is right for you, then they are in a position to be able to tell you what kind of career road map you need to follow in order to be ready for this type of job in the future.

Step #3: Applying For A Job – Evaluate The Advice

Although you may have consulted very wise people, you shouldn't just take their advice and run with it. This is your career that we're talking about after all.

Instead, what you need to do is to gather up all of the feedback that you have received and determine if your strengths and weaknesses line up with what the company that has the job posting is looking for. The last thing in the world that you want to do is to spend a lot of time, energy, and effort going after a job that is not a good fit for you.

Step #4: Applying For A Job – Identify Your Transferable Skills

I'm willing to bet that the job that you are considering applying for is not a job that you've done before. By the way, if it is then you really should be applying for a different job just to keep your career moving along.

Since you've not done this particular job before, your challenge is going to be to show the person who has been tasked with filling the job that you have the skills and the talents that will be needed to do the job. That means that it's time to do some skill mapping.

What you are going to have to do is to take a very hard look at the experiences that you've had and the training that you've received. What you want to do is to pick out the specific things that you believe have prepared you for this job. If you find this difficult to do, reach out to one of the people who gave you advice and ask them to share with you what the most important skills are that will be needed for this job.

Step #5: Applying For A Job – Rewrite Your Resume

There is no such thing as your "standard resume". You need to create a unique resume for each job posting that you go after.

What you are going to want to do is to draw on your past experiences to create a story that will tell the person who is scanning your resume just exactly why you are the best fit for the job that you are applying for.

I realize that in some cases this might start to look like it's a bit of a stretch; however, after you've repurposed your experiences and your training then you'll be able to show how all of your past successes have prepared you for the challenges associated with this new position.

I'm sorry to have to be the one to tell you this, but when you are rewriting your resume for this specific position, there may be things that need to go away. Just because you accomplished something in the past or received some award, if it does not relate to the position that you are applying for, then you need to delete it from your resume. However, feel free to add items that show your general skills such leadership, agenda setting, and your ability to create a strategy.

Step #6: Applying For A Job – Do It!

Let's face it, any of us can talk ourselves out of doing just about anything. Don't let this happen to you!

Make sure that you've done your homework and that you've researched the company that you want to go to work for. Once you've done everything that you need to do, go for it! Look at it this way, you really don't have anything to lose. The worst thing that can happen is that you don't get the job.

What will probably happen is that others will become aware that you are applying for the position and they will start to see you in a different light. This will open doors for you and who knows, you just might get the job!

Final Note

One more thing. Throughout the entire job hunt process you need to be aware of just how important time is. You would like to get things done quickly: create a resume today, apply for a job tomorrow, and have a job offer by the end of the week.

The world does not operate on your time schedule. This means that you need to sit back and take a big breath. Trust me on this: you are eventually going to get a job. It's just that it's going to happen on someone else's time schedule, not yours.

At various points in the job hunt process you are probably going to get frustrated with how slow things are moving – don't these people know that you need a job? You are going to have to be able to take a step back and pause. Let things happen according to other people's schedules – learn to work with their sense of time, not yours.

By learning to do this you'll prevent one of the things that can hold a job hunter back: seeming to come across as being too anxious. Calm down, let things move at their own pace, and you'll be amazed at how smoothly everything just seems to work out by itself.

Chapter 5

The Power Of LinkedIn

Chapter 5: How To Use LinkedIn To Find A Job

What Is LinkedIn?

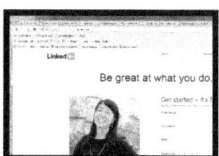

Psst. Have you heard about LinkedIn? I'm willing to bet that you probably know about LinkedIn – it's in the news every so often because it's lumped in there with all of those other social network sites. However, do you really know what anybody is using LinkedIn for?

The LinkedIn story starts way back in 2003 when it was first launched. The idea behind LinkedIn was simple enough – it was designed to be a place where working professionals could gather and exchange information. If you worked in the insurance industry, then LinkedIn was designed to put you in touch with other people who worked in insurance and even in touch with insurance companies themselves. The reasoning went that firms are always looking to hire new people and people are always looking for new jobs so why not make a web site where you could put the two together?

Needless to say, the idea was popular. As of 2011, LinkedIn had 130 Million members worldwide. The site gets over 36 million visitors each month. The big question that everyone is always asking is just exactly who is using LinkedIn?

It turns out that their members are 51% male and 49% female. Where things get more interesting is when you take a look at how much money LinkedIn members make; 30% of them make $60,000 – $100,000 while 39% make more than $100,000. Not too shabby, eh?

LinkedIn has grown to become the 2nd largest social network behind Facebook. Over at media tracking firm Nielsen Online they report that *"LinkedIn is the world's largest audience of affluent influential professionals."*

When you take a look at LinkedIn's members, 20% are senior level executives and 60% are either decision makers or have influence over purchases. Oh, by the way – these are also the people who make hiring decisions!

Executives from all of the Fortune 500 companies are now members of LinkedIn. LinkedIn continues to grow at a rapid rate. A new member joins LinkedIn every second of every day.

You are probably very familiar with Facebook. LinkedIn is quite different. There are no games, no walls, no "pokes" – LinkedIn is just for professionals who are interested in networking.

The rest of the world seems to think that LinkedIn has something good going on. When LinkedIn went public and sold their stock for the first time, their IPO said that they were worth over $6.0 billion.

Why Should You Use LinkedIn?

This is all fine and dandy and I'm sure that you wish LinkedIn the best with their continued business success. However, what does all of this have to do with your job hunt?

It turns out that it just might have a lot to do with your hunt for your first job. By joining LinkedIn (it's free to join by the way), you'll instantly get access to LinkedIn's 130M person database.

The reason that this matters is because people hire people, companies don't hire people. The more people that you can get in contact with, the better your chances of finding a person who wants to hire a person exactly like you.

Your mom knows that you are a special person and you know that you are a special person. By joining LinkedIn you have a chance to brand and position yourself as the authority online even if you are not out of college yet. What's that classic saying *"... online nobody knows that you are a dog..."*! You are unlike anyone else in the world and LinkedIn provides you with an opportunity to show everyone that.

When you sign up for a LinkedIn account, you'll get access to recruiters and hiring managers. For you see, LinkedIn is all about connecting the right people with the right jobs. Unlike job sites such as Monster.com and CareerBuilder.com, LinkedIn is a bit more refined – recruiters can get a lot more information about people before they advertise a job.

LinkedIn can be an important tool in your search for your first job. You'll have the ability to do research on target companies that you might be interested in working for. Currently, over seven million companies have company profiles on LinkedIn. What's even better is that you can see who works there and you can read blog posts, read their latest initiatives and basically learn how you can add value to that company.

When it comes to finding a job, it's all about finding out which firms are currently hiring. That's where LinkedIn comes in. As a LinkedIn member you can search posted (paid) and unposted job positions. 60% - 90% of job openings are never posted anywhere – they are filled through networking. That means that you've got to find out where the people who know about these job openings hang out and it turns out that an awful lot of them like to hang out on LinkedIn.

LinkedIn knows what side their toast is buttered on – they earn approximately 40% of their revenue from packages offered to recruiters. What this means for you is that they work very hard to make it easy for you to find open job postings. They want you to connect with firms that are doing the hiring because then you'll tell all of your friends that you found your job using LinkedIn and they'll all start to use it.

Oh, and there is one other advantage to using LinkedIn. You are a young person and all of the old people (like me) believe that you spend your days and nights doing nothing else but using social media tools like Facebook. However, it turns out that by getting in touch with a company via LinkedIn you'll be showing them that you are social media savvy. In this day and age, this particular skill is very, very important.

Why Do Some Students Have Trouble Using LinkedIn To Find A Job?

I can almost hear you now – wow, LinkedIn is such a great tool everyone must be using it to find their first job out of college, right? The answer to that question is no; however, the reasons why are a bit more complicated than that answer would lead you to believe.

There are a lot of college students who have created LinkedIn accounts and then they have not known what to do next. From their point of view getting the attention of recruiters is hard to do – the job offers didn't just start rolling in because they had created their LinkedIn profile.

Another challenge that a lot of people who are new to LinkedIn face is the simple fact that there are so many other people using LinkedIn. They don't see any way for themselves to stand out from so many other people. They also don't know how to stand out as an expert in the area that they want to get a job in.

When it comes down to applying for jobs that they've seen on LinkedIn, students can run into a number of different issues. The first is that they can't identify the hiring manager – who's actually doing the hiring? For that matter who is actually posting that job?

Since we all know that most jobs are not advertised, a big question that many students have is how do you find out about those jobs that are not being posted? They feel that they have little access to the "hidden" job market

This all comes down to the simple fact that these students are not familiar with job hunting in social media. In the end, they find themselves still typing up resumes and sending them out. If you ask them, they'll tell you that they tried social media and gave up – it was too complex.

I'm going to make sure that you are not one of those students, I'm going to show you how to use LinkedIn as an important tool in landing your first job out of college.

How Can You Use LinkedIn To Find Your First Job? (Basic Tips)

So you've signed up for a free LinkedIn account, fantastic – this is a great start! Now what?

Keep in mind that LinkedIn is a tool – it's not a magic wand. This means that you need to use it to accomplish what you want; it won't do it for you. You're going to have to use LinkedIn to meet people.

A great way to start meeting people is to join groups and make contacts. With your LinkedIn account, you will be permitted to join up to 50 groups. This might seem like a big number, but it is dwarfed by the fact that there are over one million groups that you could join!

Figure 1: Example of some of the over one million groups in LinkedIn

Remember when I said that LinkedIn makes roughly 40% of their money by selling their services to recruiters? Well, guess what – those recruiters give LinkedIn money to run ads for open positions that their customer companies are looking to fill.

When you are a member of a group, then LinkedIn knows that you are interested in whatever that group is about. LinkedIn will now start to show you paid ads for jobs that relate to that group. What's cool about these ads that are displayed within LinkedIn is that by simply clicking on the ad you'll get LinkedIn to shows you who else in your network you know at that company. This could be a handy way to get more information on what skills the company is looking for in the people who reply to the ad...

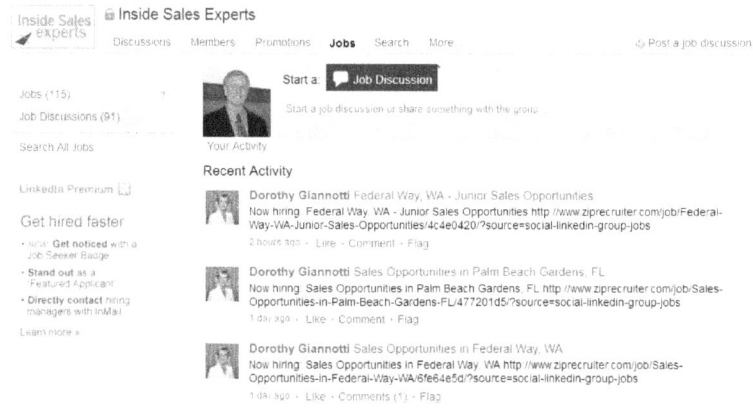

Figure 2: Many "hidden" jobs may be posted on a group's jobs tab

Not all ads that are posted in LinkedIn require the recruiter to pay LinkedIn. Every group has a job board and recruiters can post jobs to these group job boards for free. Needless to say, the jobs that they are posting are closely related to the type of group simply because the people who belong to that group are the people who will probably have the skills that the recruiter is looking for.

> Companies > Hewlett-Packard

Overview **Careers** Products & Services Insights

There's customer service. And then there's 30 million customers' service.
Laurence manages a cloud portfolio that keeps 30 million customers happy.

Laurence
What are you ready to do?
CMS Account Principal
Explore our careers. Join our revolution of doers.
France

Where Doing Gets Done
A leading French telecom operator needed a cloud portfolio that integrated software, hardware and service. And they wanted a partner—not just an IT company. So they turned to us and we turned to Laurence. With our portfolio and Laurence's drive, we've helped make 30 million customers very, very happy.

Redefining an industry—just one of the qualities that makes HP a unique place to work. We're a culture that's doing. We get things done. We have an idea and we make it happen. Our employees do it for our customers with the amazing products and services we create. And HP does it for our employees with career development, competitive compensation and benefit offerings, and opportunities that span the globe. And we're looking for the talent that will help us keep doing it.

Jobs you may be interested in...
JAVA Architect IV, HP - Mason, US-OH
Work closely with development team to remove technical roadblocks and increase development efficiencies • Oversee change control process from an ... more

Figure 3: Jobs may be listed as a part of a company's LinkedIn page

Another great place to look for jobs inside of LinkedIn is on the pages that companies have set up. Many company pages have a career section where they post jobs. Look for job ads in these company pages.

We need to keep in mind that you are not looking for any old job. Rather, there is a very specific type of job that you want – the one that is going to be perfect for you. In order to find that job you are going to need to make sure that your LinkedIn profile gets found when people are searching inside of LinkedIn for people with your specialty.

To make this happen, you are going to need to make sure that key words have been strategically located in your profile in order to make sure that you show up when recruiters do searches for people with these skills or interests. Using the right words will pull job offers to you.

Another way to make sure that you get seen in LinkedIn is to be seen as an expert by publishing constantly. Make sure that you don't just join a bunch of groups. Instead, join and contribute to the group's discussion so that you start to become known to the other group members (in a positive way!)

Make sure that your LinkedIn profile shows that you are actively seeking a job. You need to maintain top of mind awareness as a job seeker. If a recruiter visits your profile, you want them to know that they can reach out to you to discuss a position because that's exactly what you are looking for.

Finally, make sure that your network knows that you are looking for a job. The more people who know that you are on the hunt, the better. This way they'll be keeping their eyes open for you and they can let you know if they stumble across an opportunity that just might be a good match with what you are looking for.

10 Ways To Find The Perfect Job On LinkedIn (Secret Advanced Tips)

Now that you have the basics of using LinkedIn to find your first job down, let's talk about the "secret" techniques that you can use to boost your chances of being successful. These are the tips that you are not going to find anywhere else. Read on and find out how to supercharge your search for the perfect first job.

Create a career "magnet" profile.

Your LinkedIn profile is how the outside world is going to see you. What this means is that you want to take the time to build a profile that will act as a magnet and pull people who have jobs to your profile. Now the question is how best to do this?

First off, you need to be completely professional and consistent. Remember that LinkedIn is not like MySpace (does anybody still use that?), Facebook, or Instagram. We're talking about the career that you want to have here so you need to put your most professional image forward on LinkedIn at all times.

Keep in mind that everything that you do on LinkedIn brands you. What that means is that any information that you post in a group discussion or as part of your profile becomes part of how others will see you within LinkedIn. Always be thinking about how this is going to look 1, 2, or even 3 years from now.

Figure 4: How to post an update to your LinkedIn profile

The last thing that you want to happen to your profile is for people to think that it is "old" or "stale". You want anyone who sees it to believe that it represents your up-to-date information on what you're doing and where you are at. In order to make this happen, you may want to consider keeping your LinkedIn profile fresh with updates at least once a week. Do this by using LinkedIn's "Post An Update" feature that you can access by editing your LinkedIn profile.

These updates are not of the "I'm at the coffee shop" types of updates. They need to be career related. Try "Researching a new method of providing small businesses with financing during a global recession" or something like that.

Build your network

When you go to add someone to your LinkedIn network, LinkedIn will pause and ask you if you really know them. LinkedIn tells you to only add people that you know really well to your network. Balderdash!

The key to long term LinkedIn success is to have as large of a network as possible. The more people that you have in your network, the better connected you will be to people who may have a job for you. You're hearing this from me: link up with as many people as you possibly can. You never know who knows somebody who will be able to get you your first job.

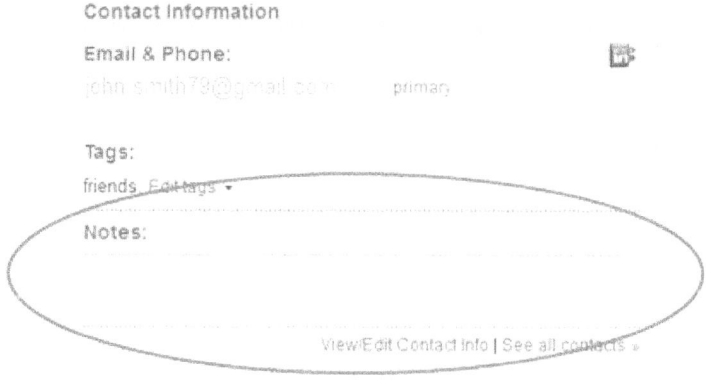

Figure 5: Be sure to keep notes on each of your LinkedIn contacts

As you are adding all of these people, it may become difficult to remember who all of them are – I have this problem. I've got some good news for you, LinkedIn can help you out. Every time that you add someone to your LinkedIn network, you can immediately view their profile. When you do this you'll see over on the right hand side of the page a small box that is labeled "Notes".

I'm going to suggest that you take the time, every time, to jot down just a few pieces of information here. I'd suggest that you put the date that you added them to your network and a word or two about why you added them to your network: they were your teacher, you belong to the same LinkedIn group, they were your roommate, etc.

This way some day in the future when you discover that this person is the person who can put you in touch with someone important, you'll be able to remember why they are in your network in the first place. That will be an important piece of information to include in the LinkedIn message that you send to them asking for their help!

The other nice thing about having a big LinkedIn network is that it means that more people can take a look at your profile. LinkedIn allows only the people in your network to see the details of your LinkedIn profile so the more of these people that there are, the more publicity your LinkedIn profile is going to get. Oh, and this is a two-way street. The more people that can look at your profile, the more profiles you can look at.

There is a small but important social issue to point out here. People can see how many connections you have – LinkedIn stops counting at 500. If you can somehow get more than 500 people to agree to join your LinkedIn network, then LinkedIn will start to tell people that you have "500+" connections and hiring managers will see you as being social media savvy.

Search for people who can hire or refer you

When you are actively looking for a job, you'll probably narrow your search to a handful of companies that you'd be interested in going to work for. This means that you are going to want to grow your network so that you have lots of people to search when you are looking to find contacts inside of the companies that you want to work for.

While you are in school, you've got a bit of a problem when it comes to growing your LinkedIn network – you just don't know a lot of people! This is a great time to connect to Mom and Dad if they have LinkedIn profiles. Go ahead and connect to other family members, fellow classmates, your professors, and anyone you connect with in a LinkedIn group. Don't worry about connecting to people that you don't know. Spamming is not a problem on LinkedIn and so most people that you encounter will be more than willing to add you to their network.

Once again, people hire people, companies don't hire people. This means that you are going to have to track down the people who are doing the hiring at the companies that you are interested in going to work for. LinkedIn has a powerful tool that will help you to do this. It's called the "Advanced People Search" tool. Take some time to play around with it and find out how it works. The time that you invest in it will turn out to be well worth it. Your free account limits you to 100 search results, in most cases that should be more than enough to get you started.

Contact the people who can help you

Now we come to a very interesting part of our LinkedIn discussion: how to get touch with other LinkedIn members. Just because you have a LinkedIn account does not mean that you can contact all 130M other LinkedIn members.

So who can you contact? Using LinkedIn terminology, the people in your network are considered to be your "first level" contacts. The good news is that you can directly contact your first level contacts. LinkedIn provides you with a button that lets you send them an email within LinkedIn.

If you are willing to pay LinkedIn for a premium account, then LinkedIn will allow you to send an email to any other LinkedIn member even if they are not a part of your network. These types of LinkedIn emails are called InMails in LinkedIn-speak.

These are emails that you can send directly, without waiting for an introduction from one of your contacts, which the site says get a 30 percent response rate. You can send 3 InMails / month with a paid LinkedIn account. There are two higher (more expensive) levels of LinkedIn accounts that give you even more Inmails.

Search the paid job postings for your perfect career

Although a lot is made of all of those jobs that are never advertised, there are still a lot of jobs that get posted on LinkedIn and you'd be a fool to not look into them. It's easy to do and well worth your time.

LinkedIn knows a lot about you based on the information that you've provided. Remember that you filled out a profile and you joined a number of groups. This all contributes to how LinkedIn views you and what kind of jobs that it thinks that you might be interested in.

Yeah, yeah – having a big computer system know that much about you might be a little bit creepy, but in this case let's consider it a good thing. For you see, LinkedIn uses its knowledge about you to pick out those jobs that are being advertised that it thinks that you might be a good fit for.

Figure 6: LinkedIn will show you jobs based on your profile

What it will do then is to present them to you in order to see if you have any interest in them. The cool part of all of this is that you really don't have to do anything. LinkedIn displays *"Jobs You May Be Interested In"* on the right side of your LinkedIn home page.

These jobs are matched to your profile and I've found them to be actually pretty accurate. The jobs that LinkedIn shows to me are a reasonably good match for the areas that I work in and the companies that I'd like to work for.

Once LinkedIn has shown you a job that you might be interested in, you can apply right through LinkedIn or through a link to their job page. Remember that this is not a newspaper, it's LinkedIn and you have some unique advantages. You can use LinkedIn to see who in your network works for the firm that is advertising the position. The other neat thing is that LinkedIn will tell you who placed the ad and that means that you can reach out directly to the hiring manager or recruiter.

Extend your reach and opportunities with groups.

LinkedIn is a community of working professionals. As a college student you are trying to crash this party and use it to connect with the right people whom you hope will be able to help you to find a job. The trick to doing this right is to meet as many people in the LinkedIn environment as is humanly possible.

Joining LinkedIn groups helps you to build your reputation … and your network. It doesn't take a genius to do the math on this one: 50 groups (the maximum that LinkedIn will allow you to join) x 1,000 people/group = 50,000 people.

Here's a little secret that LinkedIn doesn't advertise: as a LinkedIn user, normally you can only directly connect with people who are in your network. However, LinkedIn extends this rule and will allow you to directly connect with someone if both of you belong to the same group. What that means for you is that if you join the right groups, then you can use LinkedIn to connect with people who are working in the field that you want to work in and for firms that you'd like to work for.

One of the most powerful features of LinkedIn groups is that most groups have a tab that you can click on that will list job openings that group members have posted. In fact, there are some groups that are dedicated to jobs in particular areas or fields. These groups are often full of recruiters – exactly the kind of people that you'll want to be getting in contact with.

The reason that recruiters will post a job to a group's job tab is very simple. LinkedIn charges them to post a job on a job board (it costs them roughly $600). However, it's free for them to post a job on the "jobs" tab of a group.

Finally, depending on what your major is or what area you are interested in getting a job in, despite the fact that LinkedIn has over one million groups, you just might not find the right one for you. Don't despair – create your own group.

By creating a group you'll be the moderator and you can control who joins the group and what gets discussed in the group. If done correctly, this can be a great way to get some street cred in your particular career area.

Build your reputation with Answers.

A few years back there was a popular movie called "*Pay It Forward*". I won't give the movie away if you haven't seen it; however, one of the key ideas in the movie is that it's good to do nice things for people without the expectation that you'll be paid back for it.

In LinkedIn groups you have an opportunity to do your own version of "pay it forward". There are a couple of different ways to go about doing this. Let's talk about both of them.

The first is by asking really good questions in the groups that you belong to. LinkedIn gives you the ability to ask 10 questions per month. You should use all of these questions to ask the other group members questions that show that you both know your stuff and that you are always trying to learn more. Questions that can only be answered by someone with experience in the field are the best ones to ask.

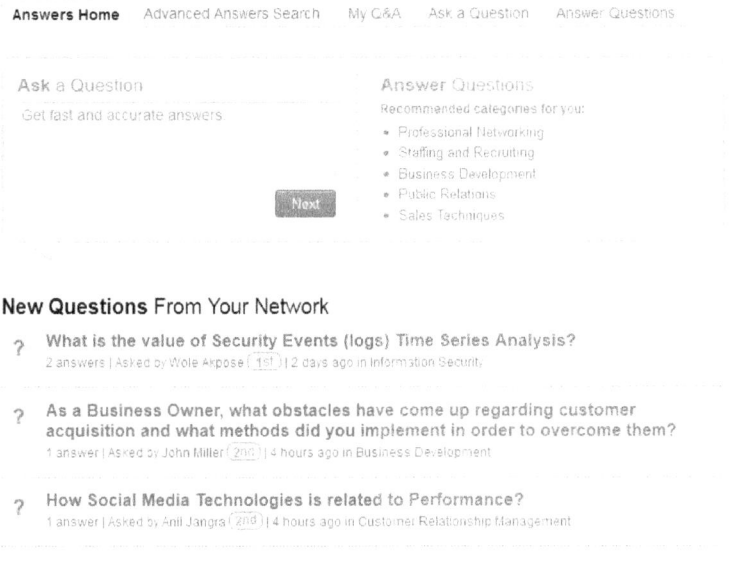

Figure 7: You can answer questions asked by other LinkedIn users

The flip side of this coin is that LinkedIn allows you to answer an unlimited number of questions per month. This is a LinkedIn feature that you really need to take advantage of. LinkedIn has a whole section called "Answers" where anyone can post a question in anyone of several different topic areas. You need to pick a topic that is close to the area that you want to work in and go looking for questions that you can answer.

You won't be able to answer all of the questions and you shouldn't try to. Instead, carefully pick the ones that you can provide an intelligent answer to. The best ones will be the ones that with a little bit of Google research you can both provide an answer and include a web link or two in order to help out the person who is asking the question.

Wonder who is going to see your answer? The person who asked the question will be grateful and other people will read the question and see your answer. This is a fantastic way for a college student to start to build an online reputation as someone who both knows their stuff and is always willing to lend a helping hand.

A little side benefit of answering questions is that LinkedIn closes questions after they have been posted for 7 days. At that time the person who asked the question is asked who provided them with the best answer.

If you do a good job of answering questions and if you answer a number of them, then you can achieve what LinkedIn calls "Expert Status" if your answer is rated the best and everyone will see that. Not bad for someone who is still in school!

Build a job hunting pipeline with Companies

If you are going to be successful in your quest to land a job with a company that you've decided that you want to work for, then you're going to have to find out as much as you can about them.

Back in the day, you'd head off to the library and hope that your library subscribed to some journal that had background information on the firms that you were interested in. Good news, you are living in the 21st Century and all of the information that you need is now available to you via your laptop.

There are over seven million companies already on LinkedIn. Many of these companies have gone to the effort to set up company profiles on LinkedIn. What's nice about these company profiles is that they often have career boards associated with them.

Figure 8: LinkedIn allows you to "follow" companies that interest you

LinkedIn gives you the ability to "follow" companies that you are interested in. When you follow a company, LinkedIn will provide you with a feed of everything that is happening at that company (press releases, articles in the news, etc.). It's almost like LinkedIn is doing your job hunt work for you!

You should use the LinkedIn information on companies to both research companies that you are interested in working for and also your connections who work there. Take the time to search the company's job posts. Even if you don't find the perfect job for you, there is a lot to be learned based on the types of people that the company is currently looking for.

Taking the time to gather all of this information will allow you to become an insider based on all of your information gathering. You can really make this pay off by reading the profiles of the people who work at the company. Don't just stop there. Read blog posts that are created by the company's employees (note that LinkedIn allows people to associate a personal blog with their LinkedIn profile). You can also read their LinkedIn activity and you'll have an understanding of what changes are happening at that company.

Get immediate job news through Signal

A relatively new LinkedIn feature is a monitoring service that allows you to stay on top of all of the changes that are happening at a given company. This tool is called "Signal".

It allows you to monitor up-to-the-minute news about jobs that have just opened up. Using Signal you'll be able to see who is hiring and this will allow you to beat out the competition when it comes to applying for open positions.

The key to getting the most out of Signal is to know how to do good searches. When you are using Signal to do a search for open positions, you'll need to use terms like "hiring", "seeking", and "looking" in order to find all of the positions that are being listed.

Find places to meet hiring managers

One final note about LinkedIn, it's not all about what happens online. It turns out that LinkedIn can point you towards events where you can meet face-to-face with real life humans.

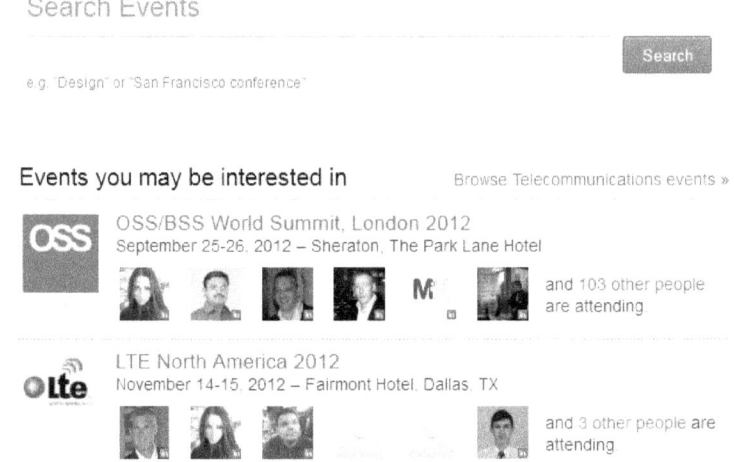

Figure 9: LinkedIn's list of events allows you to meet real people

If you take a look at an option that is located under menu option "More"->"Events" you'll find a listing of events that are occurring in your area (or any area that you care about). You can use this list of events to find job fairs, networking events, and open houses.

Once again, remember that people hire people, companies don't hire people. This means that every chance that you have to get out and meet real people significantly boosts your chances of landing the perfect job when you get out of college!

Chapter 6

How To Create A Resume That Will Get You The Interview

Chapter 6:
How To Create A Resume That Will Get You The Interview

Now that you've found the perfect job opening that somebody is advertising in order to find the right candidate, you've got to let them know that you exist. This means that you're going to have to apply for the job. This can be done either online or in person, but no matter how you go about doing it you're always going to need to have the same thing – a resume.

We're living in the 21st Century and so anything that is as old school as a resume must not really matter anymore, right? Wrong! Resumes are still important and so you need to make sure that you have a good one that will sing your praises.

The key thing to understand about a resume is that it really serves two purposes: the first is to get you the first interview and the second is to provide the interviewer with a starting point for their discussion with you.

That being said, there are a couple of other things that you need to understand about your resume. First off, unless you are Harry Potter your resume is not magical. It does not have the ability to get you a job offer all by itself. I don't care how much time you've spent picking just the right font, or laying it out perfectly on a sheet of paper, your resume won't be getting you a job.

Secondly, let's face it – you are a college student. We're going to have do some work here to even create a resume for you. It's not going to be nearly as long as or as detailed as a resume that someone who has been working for a while will have. This is a fact of life and we're going to have to find a way to deal with it.

The Basics – Suggestions For Creating Your Resume

1. **Don't Over Do It** – Need I remind you that you are still in college? This means that your resume is not going to be all that long. People are always debating how long a resume should be. I'm going to suggest that yours should be no longer than one page – this is going to be what the interviewer is expecting from you.

2. **Make It Easy To Read** – Unlike the latest mystery novel, nobody ever reads a resume from top to bottom. Instead, what they are going to be doing is quickly scanning it. This means that you are going to have to write your resume to be scanned, not read.

3. **Fonts, Fonts, Fonts** – Microsoft Word comes with something like 200+ fonts. Don't use them! Instead, pick one font to use when you are creating your resume and stick with it. If you want to play it safe you can use what everyone else uses: the Times New Roman font and choose the 12 point size. Stay away from using different sizes of your font throughout your resume because it will just end up looking silly.

4. **Paper vs. Email** – Here in the 21st Century, we don't really exchange resumes via paper any more. Therefore, you need to make sure that you convert your resume from Microsoft Word format to PDF format (I use the "Bullzip" Windows utility to do this, Google it for a free download). The PDF version is what you'll attach to emails or upload to job sites. Not everyone has

Microsoft Word or even the same version that you do – the PDF version of your resume will be what everyone can easily read and print.

One more thing that you'll have to do is to create a plain text version of your resume. Microsoft Word will allow you save your document as a "text" file. After you do this, you'll need to open it up in a text file editor such as the one that comes with Windows ("Notepad") and make sure that it's formatting is correct – generally some clean-up will be required. This is the version that you'll send to recruiters who will be using it to load your information into their computer databases. You'll also use it when you have to cut & paste your resume into online forms.

That being said, creating a paper version of your resume is still important for face-to-face meetings and job fairs. Invest in some nice heavy paper (limit your colors to white, ivory, or gray). Print your resume in black ink and take a few copies along with you everywhere you go.

5. **Highlights**: There may be specific pieces of information on your resume that you'd like to call the skimming eye of a recruiter to. I'm going to suggest that you bold it and then underline it. Some people suggest that you capitalize the important words, but I feel that it's too easy for that to look like you are yelling!

6. **Keep It Straight**: As you push and pull different parts of your resume together, you may end up with multiple columns of information. There's no problem with this;

however, if you do this then you need to make sure that everything is lined up. After you've created your resume step back and make sure that everything is in alignment with each other – anything else is going to leave your resume looking unprofessional.

7. **Both Spelling & Grammar Count**: Hey you crazy Text Message / Twitter kids – I've got some bad news for you. It turns out that when it comes to your resume, both spelling and grammar count. This means that you have to pay attention to all of those red / green / blue squiggly lines that Microsoft Word puts under the text that you've just typed in. After you think that your resume is perfect, I would suggest that you get an adult (you know, somebody who knows how to spell and understands that grammar stuff) to review it. You just might be amazed at what they are going to find!

What Goes Into A Good Resume?

Sure you've heard about resumes before, but what really goes into one? The good news is that there is no fixed format for resumes. The bad news is that there is no fixed format for resumes!

If you are an artist, a sculpture, a musician, etc. then you might want to use a very creative format for your resume to show an interviewer just how creative you can be. However, for everyone else, I'm going to suggest that you play it safe (read that as boring) and create your resume using one of the standard formats that everyone uses. This will allow anyone who is looking at your resume to quickly find what they are looking for.

A standard resume for a college student should be no longer than one page and should consist of six parts. Each of these parts will tell a slightly different story about who you are, what you've done so far, and what you want to accomplish in the future.

The six parts that should make up your resume are as follows:

1. Heading
2. Objective
3. Education
4. Professional Experiences + Qualifications
5. Skills
6. Awards, honors, and memberships

Now let's step through each of these different sections and take a look at just exactly what you should be putting into them. Remember that each section is going to have to work with the other sections in order to tell your whole story.

The Heading

The very first thing that goes into the heading section is your name. It should be your full name – no nicknames here, put what an employer would find on your birth certificate. Your name should be in all capital letters and you are going to want to center it on the page. Go ahead and make it bold – it's your name and you really want it to stand out.

Next is going to come your contact information. There will be three parts to this: a postal address, a phone number, and an email address. As simple as this sounds, there are some subtleties going on here that you are going to want to be aware of.

What postal address should you use? You can't be certain that you are going to find a job before you get out of college. Because of that, you are not going to want to use your college dorm / apartment address on your resume – you may no longer be living there when somebody decides to mail something to you. More often than not, a good idea is to use your parents' home address. The thinking is that if anything shows up there, they'll give you a call and let you know. If this is not possible for some reason and if you'll be staying in town, then you may want to consider renting a P.O. Box at your local post office. This way no matter where you live, the address on your resume will still be valid.

The phone number is another key piece of information on your resume. This must be your cell phone number (you do have one of those don't you?) The thinking here is that if a potential employer wants to get in touch with you, you want to make sure that they can and that you'll pick the phone up when they call! One other thing that you need to do is to make sure that your voicemail greeting is the kind of greeting that you'd want a potential employer to hear. Remember, it's the details that really matter!

Finally, we need to have a talk about the email address that you are going to be using on your resume. You probably have an email account that was given to you by your college. You don't want to use this address. Once again, you may be out of school and still looking for a job. Often these school email accounts get taken away from you once you stop paying tuition and so that's going to do you no good.

Instead, set up a free email account with a public provider (Gmail or Microsoft's Outlook.com are both good choices). This is the email address that you'll probably use for the rest of your career so make sure that you don't select an account name that will make you look silly (hot_guy@gmail.com or sexy_girl@outlook.com) – choose something bland and boring and you'll do fine.

Figure 10 shows an example of what a resume header could look like:

JOHN SMITH

1234 Main Street
Any Town, Maine 12345

813-555-1212
john.smith.79@gmail.com

Figure 10: Example of a resume header

Objective

The objective part of a resume has always been the source of much controversy. People like to debate whether it is necessary or not. Considering how little information you have at this point in your job hunt to add to your resume, I'm going to tell you that including an objective section is a good idea if for no other reason than it will help to make your resume just a bit longer.

So what is a resume objective anyway? The purpose of including an objective section on your resume is to tell the person who is reading your resume what kind of job you are looking for. I hope that you realize that if you are applying for a job, then the objective on your resume needs to closely match the job that the company is trying to fill!

Let me be 100% clear on this issue: every time you send your resume to somebody, you want that resume to have a hand crafted objective statement that lines up perfectly with the job that they are trying to fill. This means there is no such thing as your "standard resume". Rather, you have a template that you customize for every opportunity. Got it?

The goal of your objective statement is going to be to attempt to capture the interest of the person who is scanning your resume. Your goal should be to get them to start thinking that you might be the person that they've been looking for to fill this job.

An objective is not just a block of text. I'd rather that you think of it as a 3-layer cake (how tasty is that!) The first layer is where you inform the reader what your job hunt is all about: what kind of job are you looking for? The second layer consists of words that explain what makes you different. Finally the third layer talks about the specific skills that you have that the company is looking for in order to fill this position.

Let's say that you were going to send your resume to General Motors in order to try to get a job as an entry level car designer. Here's an example of what your resume's objective might look like:

> "An entry level auto body designer position with an automobile manufacturer that values superior design skills, quality detail work, and outstanding experience."

Let's take a look at what we have here. All three required parts are represented:

- Layer 1 – your specific objective: *An entry level auto body designer position with an automobile manufacturer*

- Layer 2 – words that show how you are different: *superior, quality, outstanding*

- Layer 3 – specific skills that you have: *design skills, detail work, experience*

Strengths

You know a lot of things. You've probably done a lot of things. However, the last thing that you want to do is to make a person who is reading your resume have to hunt in order to find out what you do best. Why not tell them upfront?

The strengths portion of your resume is designed to do this. Right up front you have a chance to tell the reader what you think that you do best. There's not a lot of room to do this, so you are going to have to be very concise.

I'd like to point out that since you are going to have to customize your resume for each job that you apply for, the list of strengths that you provide will also need to be customized for the particular job that you are going after.

You're goal in this section is simply to get the reader to start to nod their head – "Yes, those are the skills that we are looking for". You don't have to provide a lot of detail about your skills, just be very, very clear about what they are.

Here is an example of what a skills section on a resume might look like:

STRENGTHS:
- Skilled at interpersonal communications with a wide variety of people with different backgrounds.
- Ability to understand, capture, and document detailed requirements.
- Experienced in management of multiple simultaneous projects.

Figure 11: Sample strengths section of a resume

Education

How much have you invested in getting that education that you are planning on popping out of college with? $80,000? $90,000? $100,000+? No matter how much you've paid (or somebody else paid for you), it's the most expensive thing that you are going to be owning for quite some time. Your resume is a great place to show it off.

For those of you who have (or who are going to) worked hard in college, I would like to extend my deepest appreciation for your accomplishment. However, once you graduate from college, nobody really cares. What this means is that your GPA (Grade Point Average) does not belong anywhere on your resume – once again, nobody really cares about it. All that anyone will care about going forward is that you got your degree.

There are really 3 pieces of information that you are going to want to list in this area of your resume: the degree that you got, the university that you got it from, and when you got it. If you haven't quite received your degree yet, then you can list the date that you are expecting to graduate and add the magical words "Expected Graduation".

Here's an example of what your education section might look like:

EDUCATION:
B.S. in Computer Science   Washington University. St. Louis, Missouri ; May, 2012

Figure 12: Sample Education Section of a Resume

... and here's how it might look if you had not graduated yet:

EDUCATION:
B.S. in Computer Science   Washington University. St. Louis, Missouri ; May, 2013 Expected Graduation

Figure 13: Sample Education Section of a Resume Before Graduation

If you have multiple degrees, then list them in descending chronological order because the degree that you've received most recently is the one that will be of the most interest to the person who is reviewing your resume. Here's what a multiple degree section of a resume might look like:

EDUCATION:
MBA (Marketing)   University of Texas at Dallas. Richardson, Texas; May, 2012
B.S. in Computer Science   Washington University. St. Louis, Missouri ; May, 2011

Figure 14: Sample Education Section With Multiple Degrees

Professional Experiences

Are you ready for some real creativity? The experience section is where we're really going to have to become creative and transform how you've spent your time so far into documentation of activities that have lead up to you being the perfect candidate for the job that you are applying for.

I'm not sure exactly what experiences you are going to be able to draw on for your experience section. However, once again there is going to be a fair bit of customization going on here. You are going to want both the experiences that you document and the words that you use to describe them to support what you said in your objective statement.

There are going to be 7 pieces of information that you are going to want to list for each of the work experiences that you choose to include in this section. These pieces of information are as follows:

1. Company name
2. Department / Division
3. Location
4. Dates of employment
5. Title
6. Description of job
7. Qualifications

An example of what one of your experiences could look like showing all 7 parts is as follows:

EXPERIENCE:
The Gap, Tampa, Florida   2010 - 2012
Assistant Floor Manager, responsible for ensuring that all inventory was properly displayed, staff was scheduled, and to provide assistance to the floor manager on an as needed basis.
- Responsible for coordinating stock levels with other stores.
- Created new displays for Fall fashion line
- Introduced new work scheduling system that allowed staff to easily trade slots and still cover all shifts.
- Filled in for floor manager during vacations and sick days.

Figure 15: Sample experience description

The goal of your experience section is to sell yourself to the person who is looking for someone to fill their open position. You'd really like to be able to include as much experience as possible. Not only will it make you look like a more credible candidate, but it will also give the person who is reviewing your resume more material with which to have a discussion with you about.

One important thing to realize about listing your experiences is that nobody is ever going to be doing any double checking of just exactly what your title was. What this means for you is that you've got some artistic license that you can use to make your job titles look like they were all leading up to the position that you are currently applying for. Don't overdo it, but make the most of this opportunity!

Finally, dates are only a placeholder that allows the person who is reviewing your resume to understand the sequence of your different positions. I generally keep things at the year level "2010-2011" and such. Remember, that if you worked at a given job for less than a year, this approach will make it appear as though you were there for the entire year!

Qualifications

The purpose of the qualifications, which shows up on your resume as a part of your experience, is to very, very clearly state why you are the right person for the job that you want to be considered for.

You are going to want the qualifications that you list to be in alignment with your objective statement. Remember, we're not trying to list your past work experiences here, rather what we are trying to do is to come up with a list of all of the things that you've learned that may be applicable to the job that you are applying for.

What you are going to have to do is to take a very close look at the information that you have about the position that the company is trying to fill. What words did they use to describe the candidate that they are looking for?

Here is a sample job description for a Safety Manager position:

> **Job Summary**: *Manage and develop plans, programs and practices to provide for employee safety, facility*

security and compliance with Kroger best practices as well as State and Federal law. Keep upper management abreast of new developments in the area of responsibility and recommend continuous process improvements to assure budget and KPI targets are met or exceeded.

Duties and Responsibilities:

• Develop, implement and track safety training and programs

•Maintain all files related to safety training, safety certifications and licensing, inspections and audits, complaints and follow-up actions and abatements.

•Participate in new hire orientation for safety and security training.

•Develop, implement and guide the plant safety committee. The safety committee will include site inspections, accident review, accident prevention strategies and promotion of safety awareness in the facility.

•Plant liaison for security management

If this was job that you were applying for, you'd want to use the words that were used in this job description to create a list of your qualifications. What you came up with might look something like this:

- As a student aid, created and implemented best practices safety program for chemistry lab complex.

- As a research assistant at XYZ Chemicals Inc., was responsible for filing and tracking all safety inspection related paperwork.

- As a member of the university's student senate, lead committee to promote on-campus safety programs.

How you describe your qualifications is going to be almost as important as exactly what those qualifications are. What you are going to want to do is to use action words to describe your skills and talents that you used when you were performing the job.

When you add these qualifications to your job experience section, this will show the person who is reading your resume that you have the ability to accomplish any assignment that they give to you. Here is a short list of words that you might want to consider using when you list your qualifications:

obtained	administered	analyzed
taught	developed	displayed
earned	excelled	formed
handled	refined	learned
maintained	managed	organized
advanced	reviewed	supervised

The ultimate goal of the qualifications that you list is to show that you have already used the skills that are going to be needed for the position that you are applying for in your previous jobs. What you put here should answer the question "why should we hire you?"

Skills

Almost every job posting lists a set of skills that candidates will need to have in order to perform the job. The skills section of your resume gives you a very short and concise section where you can quickly list what skills you currently have that will allow you to perform the job that you are applying for.

Carefully read a number of different job postings in order to get a sense of the types of skills that employers are considering to be "table stakes" for this type of job. Things such as "Experienced using Microsoft Office" is often one and "Excellent math skills" would be items that you could include here.

Awards and Honors and Memberships

This part of your resume is the least important; however, if you've got awards or honors, flaunt them. If you spent time as part of some organization, then talk about it here. If you don't have any of these then you can drop this section.

There are really only two pieces of information required when you are listing your awards and honors: the title of the award / honor and the date that you received it. Once again, you can limit the date to just the year that you received it in. For your memberships, list the dates that you were active.

Sample Resume

Here is a sample resume where we pull together everything that we've just talked about. Note that the total length of this resume is a single sheet.

Each one of the work experiences is carefully documented and has a qualification associated with it.

Sample Resume

JOHN SMITH

1234 Main Street
Any Town, Maine 12345

813-555-1212
john.smith79@gmail.com

CAREER OBJECTIVE:
An entry level auto body designer position with an automobile manufacturer that values superior design skills, quality detail work, and outstanding experience.

STRENGTHS:
- Skilled at interpersonal communications with a wide variety of people with different backgrounds
- Ability to understand, capture, and document detailed requirements
- Experienced in management of multiple simultaneous projects

EDUCATION:
B.A. in Industrial Design   Washington University St. Louis, Missouri, May, 2015

EXPERIENCE:
The Gap, Tampa, Florida   2012 -2113
2012
Assistant Floor Manager, responsible for ensuring that all inventory was displayed properly, staff was scheduled, and provided assistance to the floor manager on an as needed basis
- Responsible for coordinating stock levels with other stores
- Created new displays for Fall fashion line
- Introduced new work scheduling system that allowed staff to easily trade slots and still cover all shifts
- Filled in for floor manager during vacations and sick days

McDonalds, Tampa, Florida   2011 - 2012
Shift Leader, managed team of 5 workers and was responsible for resolving production issues and customer complaints as well as documenting supply usage, worker hours, and safety compliance
- Interviewed and hired 5 employees
- Identified performance issue with food storage location and suggested and implemented a change that improved each shift's ability to handle rush hour crowds
- Resolved worker conflicts by listening to issues, making a decision, and then ensuring that decision was implemented
- Provided first aid treatment when required

SKILLS:
- Skilled at using Adobe Photoshop software package
- Proficient at using Microsoft Word, Powerpoint, and Excel
- Experience using Quicken Books software package

AWARDS / HONORS / MEMBERSHIPS:
2012 – Present   Member, International Auto Body Design Association
2010 – Present   Member, University Student Government
2009 – 2010   Participated in planning University's annual Homecoming Celebration Week
2009 – 2009   Manager, University Men's Wrestling Team

Figure 16: Sample complete resume

Chapter 7

How To Write A Cover Letter / Email That Will Get Your Resume Read

Chapter 7:
How To Write A Cover Letter / Email That Will Get Your Resume Read

Would you eat a jelly sandwich without any peanut butter? I don't think so. Peanut butter and jelly just go together. Likewise, a cover letter and your resume also go together.

It's not possible for your resume to introduce you or to grab the interest of the reviewer all by itself. That's what your cover letter is going to be responsible for doing. We're not talking about writing "War and Peace" here; your cover letter is going to be short & sweet and will get to the point quickly.

Just because it's short, does not mean that your cover letter is going to be lacking information. It has one job to do – sell you to the person who is going to be looking at your resume. The goal here is actually quite simple: to get the person who reads your cover letter to offer you an interview. How hard can that be?

The good news about cover letters is that are actually pretty simple to write. There are only 3 parts to a standard cover letter and we're going to cover each one of them right now.

The Introduction

If you were writing a letter home to your parents, how would you start it off? Probable you'd do it like just about everyone else and say something like "Dear Mom and Dad". Clearly we're going to want to take a different tact with our formal cover letter.

One of the most important things that you can do when you are creating a cover letter is to make sure that you send it to a real human being. Real human beings have a name and you need to use it when you are starting your cover letter.

The one thing that you don't want to do is to address your cover letter to a position: recruiter, human resources staff, director of personnel, etc. If you do that, then there is a very good chance that your cover letter and your resume are going to (1) not get read and (2) get thrown away as junk mail.

I hope that I don't even have to bring it up, but this is one place where spelling really counts. You need to spell the person's name correctly and you'll have to use their correct title.

Depending on how you plan on getting your cover letter to the company that is doing the hiring will determine what additional information you'll need. If you are going to be emailing it, then you're going to need a person's company email address. If you are going to be sending it via postal mail (do people still do that?) then you are going to need both the company's central postal address as well as the internal mail routing information for the person that you want your letter to go to. This will look something like "Mail stop #1234" or "Building A, Office 301". All of this important information can be gotten by simply calling the company and asking for it.

Now let's talk about how to start your cover letter off. I'm going to suggest that you stay away from using the phrase "Dear". You don't know the person that you are writing to and they don't know you. Instead, I'm going to suggest that you simply start your cover letter off by stating their name:

    Mr. Robert Thomas,

Next comes the first paragraph of your cover letter. There are 3 parts to this paragraph: the complement, the need, and the solution.

If you'll remember, we've talked about our example of a job description for a safety engineer position. It looked something like this:

> ***Job Summary***: *Manage and develop plans, programs and practices to provide for employee safety, facility security and compliance with Kroger best practices as well as State and Federal law. Keep upper management abreast of new developments in the area of responsibility and recommend continuous process improvements to assure budget and KPI targets are met or exceeded.*

The first paragraph of our cover letter if we were applying for this position could look like this:

> *Mr. Robert Thomas,*
>
> *As a manager for one of the most successful grocery companies, you are constantly looking for qualified, knowledgeable, and highly motivated safety engineers to monitor and maintain your facilities. These individuals not only need to be trained in the latest safety best practices, but also need to possess excellent communication skills.*

Everybody likes it when you complement the firm that they work for. In the complement part of your first paragraph you are telling them that they made a good choice when they decided to work there. This will help to set the tone for your cover letter and will make a good first impression.

Next comes the need. In this sentence, you're going to be telling the reader what kind of qualities they should be looking for in a candidate for this position. With a little luck, you'll get the reader to start nodding their head at this point in time.

Finally, we wrap things up with the solution. This is where you lay out the qualities that the person that they select to fill the position should have. Needless to say, make sure that these are qualities that you have.

The Body

The second paragraph of your cover letter is the body of the letter. It contains the information that will tell the reader that you are the right person for this job. It will explain that you have all of the qualities that they should be looking for.

Studies have shown that people need to be told what to do. Once told, more often than not they'll do what you've told them to do. That's why we're going to start the body of your cover letter off with a request for the reader to take the time to look over your resume.

We'll wrap this section of your cover letter up by pointing out to the reader that you just happen to possess the very qualities that they need in order to fill this position.

If we once again take a look at the job description for the safety engineer position, a body of the cover letter that we might create for this position would look something like this:

> *Please take the time to read my enclosed resume. You'll see that I have both the safety training knowledge and the work experience that are needed to fill this role.*

The Closing

The beauty of the closing part of your cover letter is that everything that you say in this section, you've already said before. However, this time out you'll simply use different words to say it.

The closing part of your cover letter should be started by acknowledging the challenge that the reader is currently facing. For our safety engineer position, something like this would do:

> *Mr. Thomas, Kroger needs a high quality safety team. One that will be able to ensure that your facilities are in compliance with the latest regulations and one that is well trained on safety issues.*

Note that the words that have been used in this part of the closing are positive words that you would use to describe a successful employee. Once again, with a little luck the reader's head should be nodding at this point in time.

Now for the last paragraph. You want to talk about next steps here. The last thing that you want to do is to leave things in the hands of the reader – they might decide to do nothing! Instead, you want to propose what the next step in the process could be.

You generally have two choices here, a follow up phone call or a physical visit to the interviewer's job site. Depending on the situation and the physical location of both you and the company, you could pick either one.

Assuming that you wanted to follow up this cover letter with a phone call, you could wrap up the letter with the following statement:

> *I'll give you a call next Wednesday to schedule an opportunity for us to have a more detailed discussion.*

If you take all of the parts of the cover letter that we've talked about and pulled them together, here's what the final version would look like for the safety engineer position that we've been discussing:

October 25, 2013

Mr. Robert Thomas
Kroger Corporation
1234 Main Street
Any Town, Florida   12345

Mr. Robert Thomas,

As a manager for one of the most successful grocery companies, you are constantly looking for qualified, knowledgeable, and highly motivated safety engineers to monitor and maintain your facilities. These individuals not only need to be trained in the latest safety best practices, but also need to possess excellent communication skills.

Please take the time to read my enclosed resume. You'll see that I have both the safety training knowledge and the work experience that are needed to fill this role.

Mr. Thomas, Kroger needs a high quality safety team. One that will be able to ensure that your facilities are in compliance with the latest regulations and one that is well trained on safety issues.

I'll give you a call next Wednesday to schedule an opportunity for us to have a more detailed discussion.

                                        Sincerely,

                                        Your name

Chapter 8

How to Master The Interview Process

Chapter 8:
How to Master The Interview Process

Ah, the interview – you're not going to get the job if you don't handle the interview well. However, congratulations – your cover letter and your resume got you the interview for the job that you wanted!

The way that you should look at the interview is that you almost have the job. Look, going to the effort of bringing you in and then taking time out of one or more person's day to interview you indicates that the company is willing to make an investment in you. That alone is worth something.

Now we need to have a talk about how to make the interview pay off for you. The reality of today's interview process is that more often than not it starts with one or more phone interviews and then proceeds (hopefully) to an in-person interview. You are going to have to have the skills to master both of these types of interviews.

Don't allow yourself to get all worked up about any of these interviews. Keep in mind that there is one and only one goal for each interview: to get you to the next step. The phone interview's goal is to get you brought in for an in-person interview. The in-person interview's goal is to get the company to make you an offer. It's as simple as that.

During both interviews, you're going to be talking to a person. There's really no science to their decision to move you to the next step. It's all going to be based on their gut reaction to you. If they like you, then they'll want to interact with you more during the next step in the interview process.

Preparing For The Interview – The Questions

You can use Google to search the Internet for great lists of possible questions and I'm going to suggest that you do that. What you want to do is not to try to memorize an answer for every question that you might be asked, but rather to get in the mode of answering these types of questions. In this way it's sort of like back in the day when you were doing sample questions as you prepared for the SAT or ACT – you just want to be ready.

That being said, here are the 10 most popular questions that you are going to be asked during an interview. Make sure that at the very least you have ready answers for these questions:

1. Tell me about yourself
2. What interests you about this opening?
3. What do you know about our company so far?
4. Why did you leave your last job?
5. Tell me about your experience at ___. (Fill in past job.)
6. What experience do you have doing ____?
   (Fill in each of the major responsibilities of the job.)
7. Tell me about your strengths.
8. Tell me about a time when…
   (Fill in with situations relevant to the position.)
9. What salary range are you looking for?
10. What questions do you have for me?

See Appendix D for a more complete list of 100 possible questions that you might get asked during an interview.

The Phone Interview

There's no two ways about it, a phone interview can be rough. We humans communicate so much through our body language and our facial expressions that when these are taken away from us, like during a phone interview, it can be a challenge to communicate clearly.

Logistics

The first thing that you need to worry about with a phone interview is who will be calling who. If it is at all possible, you'd like to be the person who calls the interviewer. That way you can control when the interview starts – and you can make sure that it starts on time. However, most of the time the interviewer will want to be in charge and they'll offer to call you.

Another important point to make sure that you are clear on is just exactly what day and time the call will occur. These calls are generally set up via email, so make sure that when you agree to the call you very clearly spell out the date that the call will be occurring on: "I look forward to talking with you on Tuesday, August 6th".

Likewise, you don't know what time zone the person calling you is in. When they say 2:00pm, do they really mean your 5:00pm? Once again, be very clear in the emails that you exchange to set the call up: "I look forward to talking with you at 5:00pm EST next Tuesday, August 6th."

Time

You need to not be doing anything for a full 30 minutes before the call starts. No matter if they are going to be calling you on a landline or on your mobile, you need to be somewhere nice and quiet. If you've asked them to call you on your cell phone, then you had better be in a location where you have "3 bars" or at least good reception, and a fully charged battery.

You're going to want to make sure that you won't be interrupted during the call. You'd be amazed at how often leaf blowers, fire trucks, etc. show up during these calls. To eliminate the problem with people showing up, you might want to consider taking the call from inside of your car – you should be able to control the noise level in this environment.

Stop drinking liquids at least an hour before the call starts. The last thing in the world that you want to be doing is hurrying the call up because you've got to make it to the restroom. Even worse would be if you took your mobile phone with you into the restroom and the person on the other end of the line KNEW that you had done this. Not a good image that you would be presenting there.

Make sure that you don't have anything scheduled for at least an hour after the call is scheduled to be over. If the call goes over its allocated time, you want to be able to focus on the call and not be thinking about the date or the event that you really should be getting ready to leave for.

Finally, if it is at all possible, turn off any sort of call waiting beeping feature that your phone might have. You don't want to have what you are saying start to cut out because your friend just has to talk to right now about her latest relationship issue.

Greeting

This may sound silly, but keep in mind that most of the ways that we humans communicate, body language and facial expressions, are not part of a phone call. This means that the person on the other end of the line will be making snap judgments about you simply based on the information that they are able to glean from the little things that happen during the call.

Don't answer the phone on the first ring. The person on the other end won't be ready to talk to you and you'll seem way too eager. Instead, wait for two or three rings and then pick up.

Don't assume that you know who is calling even though you do. Do not pick up the phone and just say "Hi". Instead, deliver a standard, polite, business greeting. Something like "Hello, this is John Smith". This gives the caller a chance to get their act together and confirms for them that they have called the right person. Now they can slide into what they were planning on saying and they'll feel as though they are in control of the call.

Often times the caller will ask you if this is still a good time for you. Always say yes and let them know that the call is important to you: "Yes, this time is still good – I've cleared my calendar so that we have as much time as we need."

Notes

Here's the cool thing about phone interviews – the person on the other end of the line can't see you. That means that you can consider this interview to be an open book interview! Feel free to bring as many notes to the interview as you want.

One very important note that you have to have in front of you at all times is the name of the person that you are talking to. You never know when you'll have to use his or her name and trust me, when you need to know it is exactly when you won't be able to remember it!

You also want to have the name of the company in front of you along with a print out of the job description. Do not try to have these displayed on a laptop, tablet, or a phone because technology will always let you down just when you need it the most. Print it out and go old school with hard copies.

I'm also going to suggest that you print out a list of commonly asked questions along with your answers to these questions. When the interviewer asks you one of these questions, pause for a moment as though you were thinking about the question and not scrambling to find your printed answer, then slowly and carefully read your answer to them in a naturel voice – they'll never know that you wrote it out.

Your Questions

One of the things that you need to keep in mind is that when the interviewer hangs up the phone, the last thing that you talked about with them is what is going to be in their mind. That means that you want to wrap things up on a high note.

Just about every interview ends with the interviewer asking you if you have any questions. The key here is that yes, you always have a question or two. Appendix E contains a list of good sample questions that you can ask your interviewer.

How many questions you'll have depends on a number of different factors. The first is how much time is there left in the interview? You really want to take up as much of the available tIme as possible so that when it's all over, the interviewer feels as though he or she really spent some time with you. You want them to feel as though they are now invested in having a relationship with you. This means that if you have a lot of time left, you are going to have to have a number of questions available to ask. If you just have a few minutes, you may have to limit it to just one question.

You should start out with asking your best question first. This is the question that will show that you understand the job, the company, and what they are looking for. With a little luck, it will cause your interviewer to stop for just a moment to come up with a good answer. Note that you are not trying to show off or stump them, you just want to show them that you've been listening to them and that you've done your homework.

I hope that I don't have to say this, but don't ask the interviewer about anything bad that has or is going on at the company. Things like toxic leaks, big layoffs, or lawsuits should be considered to be off limits for you and your questions.

Listen to the answer that the interviewer gives you to your question. In an ideal world, what you would like to do is to ask your second question based on something that they said in their response to your first question. The reason for this is because it will show that you were both listening and thinking about what they had to say. This will be taken as a great compliment.

Ultimately this gets to the heart of a successful phone interview. Nothing that you say is going to wow and amaze your interviewer. Instead, your goal should be to get them to talk as much as you can. The reason for this is because if at the end of the hour or so that you talked, if they did most of the talking then you had less chance to make a mistake and they'll have a happy positive memory of the interview because they got to do all of the talking!

Standard Tips For Successful Interviewing

Learn About The Company

We all know how to use Google, right? Then there is no excuse for you to walk in the door to your next interview without having your head full of knowledge about the company that you are trying to get a job with.

Things that you should take the time to research include any press releases that the company has put out (if it was important enough to them to release a press release, then it's important to you), the history of the company, who's running the company (Chairman, CEO, COO, CMO, CIO, etc.), any lawsuits, what their share price is currently at & where it's been over the last year, what products they sell, and what promotions or sales they are currently running.

What you want to make sure that you do is to get ready to handle any questions that might get thrown at you during the interview about your knowledge of the company. This is an easy way to impress your interviewer. You can also use the information that you gather to customize the questions that you'll be asking your interviewer (see Appendix E).

Arriving For The Interview

Let's assume that that phone interview thing went well for you – congratulations! Now it's time to gear up for the in-person interview and this is a completely different beast.

The first thing that you need to realize is that the interview starts long before you reach the building where the interview is going to take place. Your mental attitude is going to play a major role in how other people see you. Make sure that you are "up" for this interview. I don't care how nervous you may be -- don't you dare do any drugs or any drinking before the interview!

Make sure that you know who you will be meeting with. This means that you know both their name and how to spell it. If you know their desk and mobile phone numbers, then that's even better.

Arrive for the interview early. You are going to want to be in the lobby of the building where the interview is going to take place at least 15 minutes early. However, you are going to want to be in the parking lot of that building at least 30 minutes early. Remember, just because you get there early, you don't have to get out of your car until it's time to go in.

The first people that you'll often meet when you arrive for your in-person interview will be the front desk security guards. These folks will more often than not be working for a firm that has the contract to provide security for the building and they really couldn't care the least about you.

Be nice and polite to them – they can't really help you, but they can cause you hassle and harm. Understand that their job is to follow procedures and so you need to do what they tell you to do. Generally speaking, this consists of signing in, perhaps getting your photo taken, and putting some sort of badge on the top half of your person. Put the badge on no matter how bad it looks – you can always move it later on, but for now just do what the guards tell you to do.

The guards will probably now ask you who you are here to see if they haven't already asked you. Provide them the name and spell it for them if it is long or unusual. It will be even better if you can provide them with your contact's desk number so that they don't even have to go to the effort of looking it up.

Somebody will come down to the lobby to meet you. This is a good time to shake hands with this person and introduce yourself. Make sure that you get their name – you don't want to be fumbling for it later on.

As you walk from the lobby to where the interview will take place, you'll have a chance to make light conversation with the person that you are walking with. Seize the opportunity. If possible, don't talk about school – they may forget that you are still in school and may see you as a young adult, not a student. Good topics include the weather – ask questions about how it has been, how long the person has worked for the company – and where they worked before they were here, and questions about the surrounding geographical area that the person might know about.

Making A Good First Impression

I'm sure that you've heard the old expression *"You never get another chance to make a good first impression."* I hate to tell you this, but it's true.

The person who is going to be interviewing you does not know you. This means that all 5 of their senses are going to be on full alert when they meet you for the first time. They are going to be trying to size you up. They won't be waiting to hear how clever your answers to their questions are, they will have already formed an opinion of you and they'll spend the rest of the interview trying to get your answers to fit that impression.

What all of this means is that you need to make the best first impression that you can. There are a lot of things that you are going to have to do, so here's a checklist for you to follow:

1. **Lose The Piercings / Jewelry / Tattoos:** I understand that the various pieces of metal that you may have stuck into your body are really a part of who you are. However, when you are interviewing for a job they are a distraction and that's the last thing that you need right now. Remove the piercings (especially tongue studs – yes, they will be seen), tone down the jewelry (guys – get rid of it), and cover up any tats that you might have. There will be time to introduce all of these things AFTER you get the job.

2. **Dress Professionally:** Forget that individuality thing, now is the time to conform and fit in. What your goal needs to be is to look like someone who already works for the company. You want the interviewer to see you as an employee. This isn't as hard as it may seem. What you need to do is to determine what people who work in this industry dress like, and then dress just a little bit nicer than they do for your interview. What we're talking about here is a suit and a tie for men, a dress or pants for women.

3. **Show Your Self-Confidence**: I really don't care if you knees are knocking together and you feel as though you might pass out – you are going to want to exude a sense of supreme self-confidence. One way to do this is to dress in dark colors. These dark clothes will convey a sense of power to your interviewer and you will be perceived as being self-confident even if you really are

not. Choose your clothes based on powerful colors including black, dark blue, gray, dark gray, or brown.

4. **Make It All Work Together**: Speaking as a fashion challenged guy, this is where many of you, like me, may need some outside help. You are going to want to make sure that your entire outfit works together. Yep, we're talking about being color coordinated. If you are a guy, this means that your tie, belt, shoes, and your socks all need to go with each other. Keep your shirt simple – choose a plain white shirt (can't go wrong there!) and pick a tie with red as its main color. No clever patterns or Disney characters please. Women generally do a better job of this matching thing, but they need to make sure that their shoes, blouse, and dress or skirt all go together.

5. **Posture**: This is an important part of who you are and it can be the most difficult skill to master. You need to be aware of what your body is telling other people. Specifically, you are going to want to hold your head up high and keep your shoulders held back. This will make you look as though you have both strength and stability and are very secure. These are qualities that the company is looking for when they hire people.

6. **A Good Handshake**: We generally don't think about our handshake, but since the person who is interviewing you knows so little about you and since it is our custom to greet people by shaking their hand, your handshake will go a long way in helping to form the initial impression of you. The good news is that a handshake

is something that you can practice and get right. Work with your friends and family members and get their feedback: too soft, too hard, too clammy, too long, too short, etc. Find out, change, and repeat. Get this right and you'll be off to a great start with your interview.

7. **Eye Contact**: You would be amazed at just how much information human beings communicate via our faces. A big part of this communication comes from our eyes. Here's what you are going to want to do: look your interviewer directly in the eyes. Now you do need to be careful here, if you stare at them for too long, then you are going to come across as being sort of creepy. What you are going to want to do is to strike a balance. Look at them in the eye while they are talking to you. When they stop, look away as though you are thinking of an answer to their question (and you may actually be doing this), then look back into their eyes and answer their question. It really is that easy to do this right.

How To Give A Great Interview

Enough of this beating around the bush stuff. Let's talk about what you need to do during the actual interview. This all might strike you as being very similar to an actor playing a role in a stage play, and you'd be right. You are playing the role of the perfect candidate for this position and the award that you'll get for a great performance is a job offer.

- **Always Think Before You Speak**: The kind of talking that you do during an interview is quite different than the type of talking that you do every day with a friend. When you are asked a question, pause and think about the answer that you are going to give. Is there anything that you might be getting ready to say that you'll regret later on? How can you work as many words and phrases that your interviewer has used into your response so that they'll feel as though it's the same answer that they would have given? Finally, consider how your answer is going to change what the interviewer thinks about you – every answer will change their opinion, will it go up or down?

- **Speak The Truth**: Remember that your interviewer doesn't know you. This means that all 5 of their senses (and maybe all 6 of 'em) are on full alert when they are talking with you. If you don't believe what you are telling them or if you are trying to fool them, they're going to know it. Some body motion on your part will give you away and they'll get the message that they can't trust you. The interview will effectively be over.

- **Always Be Positive**: We all have things that we don't like or people that we don't think highly of. An interview is not the place to discuss either of these things. You need to be happy, happy, positive, positive during your interview. Remember, the interviewer is trying to determine if they want to work with you. A negative person is a downer and nobody wants to work with them. In every question that you are asked, look for the most positive angle and use that to form the basis of your answer.

- **Names Mean Everything**: In some books that you'll read you'll see instructions that tell you to always refer to your interviewer as "Sir" or "Ma'am". Don't do this –

in the 21st Century nobody speaks this way and you're just going to make your interviewer feel old. In the real world, when we talk to people we address them using their first name. You should do this. Your interviewer is expecting this and they'll appreciate that you've taken the time to remember what their name is. There is no more pleasing sound to a person than the sound of their own name. Just be careful to not overdo it – if I hear my name too many times in a row, it will seem odd or strange.

- **Speak Clearly & Drop The Slang**: Hey you texters and tweeters, hear me and hear me good: an interview is no place to be using the slang phrases that are so much of your everyday life. Remember that your interviewer is going to be listening to your every word and using each word to form an opinion of you. That means that you need to speak clearly and use proper English. What words need to go away you ask, here's a partial list:

Do Not Say This	Say This
I'm cool wit dat	I'm OK with that
my peeps	my friends
that's phat	that's very nice
ain't	is not
yah	yes
I been	I have been

- **Answer Questions**: We've already talked about the types of questions that you may be asked during an interview (see Appendix D for a complete list of 100 possible questions). Now we should talk about how best to answer those questions. Here's the key: keep your answers short and to the point. Nobody wants to hear a long rambling answer. Remember the whole goal of this interview is to sell yourself to the person who is interviewing you. You're not going to do this if you bore them with your answers to their questions. Make your answers concise and intelligent and deliver them with confidence and be direct.

Things NOT To Do During An Interview

Just before we wrap this part of the discussion up, let's cover one last thing: the things that you should not bring up during an interview. Some of these might seem obvious; however, others may not be something that you'd normally think of. Let's make sure that none of them come back to bite you…

- **Don't Ask About Vacations**: How many vacation days the company will provide you with each year is a good question; however, not during an interview. If you ask then you are going to come across as a slacker who really doesn't want to work that hard. Wait until they offer you a job and you start to negotiate before you ask about vacation time.

- **Don't Ask About Promotions:** Look, you don't even have this job yet. Keep the focus on the current position and don't confuse the issue by trying to find out what it takes to move on to the next position. If you get the job, you can find out how this works then.

- **Don't Turn The Weakness Question Into A Positive:** The person who is interviewing you is (probably) not stupid. If you tell them that your greatest weakness is that you just work too hard, they are going to know that you are full of it. Everything that you say after this will be suspect.

- **Don't Lie:** You are a bad liar and if you try to exaggerate your experience or fib about your accomplishments, your interviewer is going to know that something is up. You won't be able to keep track of your lies and you'll eventually slip up.

- **Don't Ask If There's Any Reason You Shouldn't Be Hired:** This is the silliest question ever. Some interview books will tell you to do this so that you'll know where you stand, but don't. The interviewer probably doesn't know the answer and you'll just be leaving them with a negative impression of you in their brain as the interview wraps up.

Secret Tips For Successful Interviewing

Ok, now we're done talking about all of the standard things that you need to master in order to have a successful job interview. Feel free to stop reading this chapter right now. Stop, that is, if you have no interest in learning the secret Jedi mind-tricks that you can use to literally make the interviewer want to give you the job that you are interviewing for.

What too many students forget is that the job is not necessarily going to be offered to the candidate who is the smartest or who has the most relevant work experience. Instead, it's going to be offered to the person that the interviewer has the best feeling about.

Yes, I said the "f" word – "feeling". I hope that that seems sort of squishy to you because it is. It's not something that any of us can really define very well and that's why so many students do a poor job of creating a good feeling about themselves in the mind of their interviewer.

It turns out that with a few simple techniques, you can leave your interviewer feeling like he or she has known you for years. This level of familiarity is a critical part of making them "like" you and therefore want to offer you the job that you are interviewing for.

Before we get started, I need to get you to agree with me on one simple point: we are all still animals. As fancy and refined as we may like to think of ourselves as beings, we still share many of the very basic traits that our ancestors had possibly millions of years ago.

One of these traits that we just can't shake is the habit of reaching a snap decision about whether we like someone when we met them for the first time – especially during an interview. I can't stop this from happening, but I can teach you how to use it to your advantage.

There is actually a very good reason why we rush to make snap decisions. Our ancestors oh so long ago had to be able to very quickly make life and death decisions. The ones who did this well lived and passed their genes on to us. That's why we're so good at making those fight or flight decisions.

Couple this tendency to make snap judgments with one of the side-effects of living in the 21st Century, our short attention spans, and you'll start to understand why your interviewer will have made their mind up about you before you even get a chance to answer your first question. Studies have shown that the average person's attention span these days is roughly 30 seconds. That's not going to leave you very much time to win the job!

If you don't believe me, and some of you may not, then try a little experiment. Try to fix your attention on something for 30 seconds. Even if you are able to do this, after about 10 seconds or so your eyes are going to be begging you to look somewhere else because they have become very, very bored.

Where this is all leading to is a simple fact of life, you will capture the attention of your interviewer with your likability, but you will hold it with the quality of rapport that you establish with them.

Hmm rapport, that term seems familiar, but what does it really mean? Over at Wikipedia, they define rapport as:

> **"Rapport** *occurs when two or more people feel that they are in sync or on the same wavelength because they feel similar or relate well to each other."*

It turns out that we humans like people who are like us. If you can establish rapport with the person who is interviewing you, then they'll like you. Liking you is a big step towards offering you the job that you are interviewing for.

In order to build a sense of rapport with your interviewer, there are 3 different things that you can do. Each of these by itself is powerful; however, when you combine all three of them together, you'll be virtually unstoppable.

The three things that you can do that will make virtually any interviewer decide that they like you on the spot are as follows:

1. Eye contact

2. Become a chameleon.

3. Grab their imagination.

Eye Contact

Exactly how important is making good eye contact with your interviewer? It turns out that it's very important! A study that was done way back in 1967 revealed how humans communicate with each other. Here's what the researchers found out about how we communicate information to someone else when we are talking with them:

- 55% - body language,
- 38% - vocal tone
- 7% - actual words

Using this new information, think about what you do when you meet someone. Where do you tend to look? What does this make the person think about you? It turns out that it's all about the eyes – or if you don't look into their eyes, then it's all about why you can't look them in the eyes!

When you arrive for an interview and you meet the person who will be interviewing you, you should right way look them straight in the eye when you greet them. This shows openness, and will instantly reduce their urge to flee. After all, who really wants the person who is going to be interviewing them to flee?

It's not always easy to remember to do this. Therefore, I have a helpful little tip for you that should help you to remember to do this. Every time you meet someone today ask yourself "What color are their eyes?" This will automatically make you look into their eyes and they'll feel that you are truly connecting with them.

Good eye contact needs a few additional helpers to be the powerful tool that it can be. When you are talking with your interviewer, make sure that your hands are open and clearly holding nothing threatening – this further reduces a person's initial hostility towards you.

Don't forget to smile all of the time during your interview. This is a critical part of the initial greeting. Make it a real smile, not a forced grin. A natural reaction to a real smile is to smile back at you and that has to be a good thing.

This next part might sound silly, but we all need just a little bit of help in improving how we smile. Go home tonight and get in front of a mirror and say the word "GREAT". Do this a number of times and see what a large natural smile it produces!

Become A Chameleon

This is an important one. Think about the people that you tend to get along with and like the best. Why do you click with them? It is a sad fact of life but we tend to like those people who are the most like us.

Have you ever seen people when they are hanging out with family or friends? Watch how their bodies move. They tend to mirror the people that they are talking with. Their bodies are in the same position as the people that they are talking to.

Likewise, have you seen adults get into a confrontation? What did their body language look like? You got it – their body positions made them look like direct opposites.

When it comes to your interview, you are going to want to basically mirror the body position of the person who is interviewing you. CAREFUL: this is dangerous stuff that we're talking about here. You don't want to let them know that you are doing this or else it will look like you are mocking them.

What this means is that you need to adjust your body position to match theirs very, very slowly. Ease into the position that they are currently in. When they switch positions, take your time and flow into their new position. By doing it slowly and very smoothly, they'll never notice what you are doing. However, they will feel a real sense of connection to you even if they don't know why…

It's always a good idea to try doing this before you find yourself in a job interview. Next time you are in a meeting or are meeting with friends, start to match the person sitting across from you and see what happens. They should warm up to you. Then start doing the opposite and see what happens. You should see a cold wall start to rise. How cool is that?

Grab Their Imagination

This is another big one. If you are applying for a job that a number of other candidates are being considered for, you've got a problem – you are standing in the middle of a crowd.

After someone talks with you, can they remember anything that you said? Are your conversations boring? Are you boring?

We can't have this boring stuff going on during a job interview otherwise you'll just get lost among all of the other people who are vying for the job. We communicate by using our 5 senses. Words are just tools that we use to describe what we have already felt.

Let's see what we can do to make what you say more memorable. How would you describe the dinner that you had last night to someone that you just met: *"I had heated up lasagna"* or *"I had layer after layer of melt-in-your-mouth noodles that were swimming in a sea of tomato sauce and garlic."* Which description would you remember?

When you meet the person who will be interviewing you for the first time you'll need to capture their imagination by talking about something that they can imagine using one or more of their senses. Weather is a great way to capture their senses: "I touched the hood of my car after I got out and had to jump back when I burned my finger" or "I had to drive with the window down so that the windshield didn't fog up and it got so cold in my car that I couldn't feel my nose".

4 Key Characteristics of "Likeability"

In the end, we want the person who is interviewing us to walk away from the interview feeling that they like us as a person. This is much more valuable than anything else that will happen during the interview.

In the end, how likeable we are is going to be based on four different factors that the interviewer will walk away from our interview with:

1. Friendliness

2. Relevance [We like people who are like us]

3. Empathy [our ability to step into their skin, feel what they feel, comment on how they feel]

4. Be Real [if we seem to be genuine or fake]

The meaning of communication lies in the response it gets. It is 100% up to you whether or not your own communication succeeds during your job interview. Good luck!

Chapter 9

How To Stand Out From Everyone Else Who Is Looking For The Job That You Want

Chapter 9:
How To Stand Out From Everyone Else Who Is Looking For The Job That You Want

We've already talked about how to make sure that you come across looking great during your interview, but the one thing that we didn't talk about was what you needed to do in order to not look like everyone else who will be interviewing for this job.

I would argue that the worst thing that you could do during a job interview, outside of making the interviewer angry, would be to be forgettable. Blah. Colorless. If you were boring and forgettable during the interview, then why would I ever ask you to come and work with me?

This is a tricky problem to solve. If you do it wrong, then you'll be memorable for all of the wrong reasons. That's why each of the following techniques needs to treated like the fragile things that they are – if you're too rough with them, they will break and you won't get what you want.

Know the company, know their products

If you really want to make a lasting impression on your interviewer, a very easy way to do so is to come across as being smart. I'm not talking about college book smart here, but rather smart where it counts.

There are three types of knowledge that you can demonstrate throughout the interview that will impress your interviewer: knowledge of what the job will require you to do, knowledge of what the company does and the issues that it is facing, and knowledge of the industry and the challenges that it is dealing with at this time and in the future.

You would expect that every interview candidate will have at least a passing knowledge of the company and its products. Let's call this a Google-level of knowledge.

What you want to do is to dive in deeper so that you'll be able to impress your interviewer with your understanding of how their customers use their products to solve industry related problems.

When you can hold a substantive conversation about an industry related topic for 15-20 minutes with your interviewer, they will remember you. If you can actually tell them something they didn't know, even better.

By doing this you'll start to look like you've already been working in their industry. This is going to make you stand out from everyone else that they talked to who were clearly just starting out. It will make it much easier to both remember you, and select you for the job.

Tell a great personal story

We human beings sure do like our stories. Since back in the days where our great-great-great-great grandfathers were all sitting around a campfire swapping stories about the latest hunt, to today's rash of reality-based television shows, it's always been about the story.

What this means for you is that every time that you get asked a question during your interview, you have a unique opportunity to make yourself memorable. What you don't want to do is to respond with a one-sentence answer.

Instead, when appropriate, you are going to want to provide your interviewer with a story that answers the question that they asked. Remember what goes into a good story: a situation, a challenge or issue, characters, action, and an outcome.

You need to be very careful here. This way of becoming memorable is most definitely a double edged tool. If you tell too many stories, they'll get all jumbled up in your interviewer's head. If you take too long to tell your stories, then the interviewer may become frustrated because they aren't making it through all of the questions that they wanted to ask you.

In order to make this approach for being memorable work out, you need to plan ahead. Prior to the interview map out two or three key stories that show you in your best light – perhaps dealing with difficult people, situations, or customers. Plan your words and how the story plays out so that it shows you in the best light possible.

Work on telling the story in a way that seems unhurried, but ends up not taking that long. Pick what colorful words you are going to include in the story so that when you tell it for real, it paints an unforgettable picture in the head of your interviewer.

Show lots of enthusiasm

Your energy level is going to spill over onto your interviewer. No matter if you are their first interview of the day or their 15th, if you come in with a positive attitude and a lot of enthusiasm, then they can't help but get pumped up.

You are going to want to come across as being enthusiastic about the opportunity. Make sure that you smile, laugh (not nervously), and that you shake hands with gusto.

The interviewer will remember the energy that you brought to the interview as much as anything that you say during the interview. Your enthusiasm will make the impression that you want to leave with him or her.

Look memorable

Once again, we're on risky ground here, but the benefits probably outweigh the risks if you do this one correctly. I know that we've already talked about how you should dress for the interview, and that information is still good.

However, now I'm going tell you that if you've followed all of my advice, you're going to end up looking like everyone else who is interviewing for the job. That's why we're going to want to shake things up just a little bit.

What I'm talking about here is adding an unexpected flash of color somewhere on your outfit. Not too much – if you overdo this one, then you'll end up being remembered for all of the wrong reasons.

Women have it easier: they've got more color options. It could be a colorful purse, an arresting necklace, etc. Men will struggle a bit more. It might be a colorful pocket square. Don't overdo it!

Sound bites

You already know many of the questions that you are going to be asked. What this means, of course, is that prior to the interview you can prepare your answers for these types of questions.

However, why stop there? When you are planning how you will respond to the anticipated questions, why not take the extra time to craft a reply that will be truly memorable?

Politicians know how to do this very well. They realize that what they say will be trimmed down to fit into a nightly TV news show, so they create memorable phrases. You need to do the same.

You need to create sound bites that will ring in your interviewer's ears long after the interview is over. An example of a sound bite that an interviewer would remember would be if you were interviewing for a programming job and you told your interviewer that *"... I was then able to produce in a single night the same amount of code that it would have taken a team of programmers a week to create..."*.

Alternatively, if you were applying for a business position, you might say something like *"... my report is still being used to target leads, 3 years after I left the company..."* Keep it short and simple and your words will be remembered long after you leave.

Really smile

You would be amazed at how little smiling actually occurs in the average workplace. If you show up and smile at everyone that you meet, you will be memorable.

Don't overdo it. If the smile never leaves your face during the entire interview, your interviewer is either going to think that you are an idiot or they are going to think that you got one Botox shot too many before you showed up for the interview.

A pleasant smile that you share with each person that you encounter during the interview process will go a long way to establishing you as the type of person that they want to work with. This is easy to do, you just have to remember to do it.

Chapter 10

How To Follow Up The Interview So That You'll Be Remembered

Chapter 10:
How To Follow Up The Interview So That You'll Be Remembered

Congratulations – you feel that you nailed the job interview! Now what? At the end of the interview, did the interviewer jump over the table that separated the two of you and hand you both a job offer and a pen to sign it with? No? I thought so.

Job interviews don't end with a job offer (normally). Instead, the interviewer needs to talk with the other people that you've met to get their feedback on what they think of you. There may also be other candidates that they want to talk to before they make their final decision.

Hmm, it looks like you have a bit of a dilemma here. If you don't find a way to keep the interviewer's attention focused on you, then they may forget about you and you won't get the job. It looks like we're going to have to come up with a way to make sure that you'll be remembered – in a positive way.

It's very easy to be remembered for all the wrong reasons. If you want this to happen, then just pick up the phone and start calling your interviewer every day asking "Have you made a decision yet?" I can assure that they will make a decision and they won't be picking you.

Instead, we're going to have to a bit more clever here. What we're going to want to do is find ways to be remembered that won't come across as being annoying. The good news is that I know how to do this and I'm going to share it with you.

Get A Business Card

This starts before the interview is even over. Get a business card from every person that interviews you. The reason that you're going to want this is because it will have all of the different ways that you can contact this person long after the interview is over.

If somebody doesn't have a business card, then before you leave find a secretary or an administrative assistant who can look up that person's phone number and email address.

I prefer to be a little bit more proactive. Once I have one person's contact information, all I need is the last 4 digits of anybody else's office phone number (the first 6 digits will be the same for everyone) and a confirmation of the correct spelling of their email address. I'll whip out a pen and ask for their office number and then, since I've looked at other employee's email addresses, I'll say "Would I be correct to assume that your email address is…" When they confirm it (and the spelling of their name), I'm good to go. Clearly you are going to have to remember to bring pen and paper with you to the interview.

Immediately after you leave the interview, like when you are sitting in the rental car in the parking lot, whip out the business cards that you got and write on the back of each one everything that you remember about that person. I like to try to keep my business cards in the order that I receive them so that I do a better job of remembering who's who.

Ask About Next Steps Before The Interview Is Over

Once again, this is a step that you need to take before the interview wraps up. You need to ask the decision maker what their next steps are and what kind of timeframe they are working with.

One of the reasons that you are going to want to do this is because you'll want to know if too much time has passed. If they say that they'll be getting in touch with in a week and 9 days have gone by, then you'll want to be getting in touch with them.

By asking this question at the end of the interview you'll impress the interviewer that you are professional and that you are trying to fit the interview follow up into your obviously busy schedule. This is a good thing and it will give you material to discuss when you follow up with them: "You had mentioned that you would be making a decision in 5 days and I had not yet heard from you..."

Send An (Electronic) Thank-You Note

Immediately after your interview you are going to want to send a thank you note to everyone who interviewed you. Remember, when you walked out the door after the interview, everyone started to forget about you. The purpose of the thank you note is to cause them to start to think of you again.

There have been many discussions regarding if you should send an email or go to the extra effort to send a postal letter. Let's put this one to bed right now – send an email. Postal emails will take too long to arrive (long after the actual interview) and lots of people don't actually get postal mail at the office any more so there's a good chance it will never reach its target.

Timing is everything with this email. You need it to show shortly after the interview, but not too quickly. You should not send the thank you on the day of the interview. The people that you've interviewed with are already thinking of you because they just talked to you.

What you really want to do is to have your thank you email sitting in their inbox when they arrive at work the next day. This is a new day and they had not been planning on thinking about you, but now that they've read your thank you, they can't help it. An added bonus is if they are making a hiring decision the day after your interview – you'll be the first one that they think of!

This now leads us to an important part of this discussion: what should you put in your thank you note? Good news, there's a formula for this – there should be four parts to your job interview thank you email.

The first part is where you thank them (after all, it IS a thank you note). Thank them for their time and let them know how nice it was to meet them.

The second part is where you ask a good question. Your goal here is to ask a question that shows the interviewer that you heard everything that they told you, and that you've been thinking about it. One of my favorite post-interview follow questions has always been:

> *"Thanks for taking the time to explain to me what this part of the company does. After the interview, it occurred to me that I had forgotten to ask you an important question. Can you tell me who you believe your primary competitor is in this space?"*

The third part is where you can start to build towards your next meeting with the interviewer. Something along the lines of "*I hope to see you again soon*" should do the trick.

Finally, in the fourth part you sign the email. If you have a standard email signature, delete it. Instead, replace it with a simple name and cell phone number. Don't use your formal name, use the name that everyone uses when they talk to you ("Tom" instead of "Thomas").

Ask To Connect Via LinkedIn

This is a great idea, but you need to be careful how you go about doing it or it will come across as being somewhat creepy. The basic idea is that you've formed a relationship with the person that interviewed you no matter if you get the job or not.

You are going to have to plant the seed during the interview. Come right out during a lull in the interview and tell them that you are in the process of trying to grow your LinkedIn network and you'd like to be able to add them to your network. Ask them if it would be ok?

This person is someone who works in an industry that you want to work in and so they just might have some contacts that could prove to be valuable to you later on.

Assuming that they were agreeable to joining your LinkedIn network then the one thing that you definitely don't want to do is to use LinkedIn's generic request for someone to join your LinkedIn network. This is a case where you're going to have to create a short personal request for them to join your network.

I would suggest something that reminds them that they agreed to join your network. An example would be:

> *Paul,*
>
> *Thanks for agreeing to help me grow my LinkedIn network. Accept this invitation and we'll both have larger networks and that has to be a good thing!*
>
> *-   John*

Provide Valuable Information

This is one of my favorite techniques. Sometime after you've sent the thank you note and before they promised to have a decision for you, you can send another email.

The purpose of this email is two-fold. The first thing that you are going to be trying to accomplish is to show your interviewer that you listened, you understand their needs and their challenges, and here's how you can help them address their problems. You might want to also concisely remind the interviewer of what you've accomplished in the past.

The second part is the valuable part where you get to show your stuff. During the interview the interviewer(s) told you about things that are going on at the company right now. New product launches, sales efforts, competitors, etc. What you need to do is to fire up Google and find some very current information that relates to what they told you.

In the second part of your email you are going to want to provide the information that you've uncovered in a causal "*I ran across this and though you might be interested in it*" way. What it shows is that you are already working for them and they haven't even offered you the job yet!

So what would one of these emails look like? Here's a quick example to give you an idea of what you should be writing:

> Paul,
>
> I've been spending some time thinking about what we discussed during my interview last week . You did a great job explaining the branding challenges that the company will be facing in the next 12 months. I've had a chance to work on several branding campaigns for student organizations that I have been involved in and I understand some of the challenges that you'll be facing.
>
> I ran across an article that talked about how Coca-Cola dealt with a situation that seemed to be similar to the one that you are facing. Here's the link if you are interested:
>
> http://designshack.net/articles/graphics/pepsi-vs-coke-the-power-of-a-brand/
>
> Thank you,
> John Smith

Solve The Drag-Out Problem

Sometimes the interviewer just doesn't get back to you. They go quiet and you quietly go crazy waiting for them to tell you yes or no. Be very careful – if you annoy them, you may talk yourself right out of a job.

When you are either past the date that they said that they'd be making a decision or 9 working days later (sort of a made-up number, but it seems to work) you can make a call to the person who interviewed you.

The purpose of this call is not to harass the person who will be deciding who they want to hire. You need to assume that for whatever reason, they have not made a decision yet. If that's true, then you want to make sure that they remember you in a positive way.

When you make contact with the interviewer, introduce yourself and remind them that you interviewed with them and tell them what job you were going for. It's been awhile and they may have talked to a lot of other people about other jobs.

Tell them that you just wanted to check in with them to see what their next steps were going to be and if they had come up with a timeline. Do not point out that they've apparently already blown by the original date that they had mentioned during the interview.

If more time passes after this call and no response is forthcoming, then it's time to send an email. Make the text of the email similar to what you told them in your phone call.

If things still drag out – and sometimes they do – alternate between phone calls and emails roughly once a week until they finally provide you with an answer.

Don't worry about coming across as being too pushy. As long as you are not contacting them too often, your actions will be seen as showing your interest and your drive. Both of these characteristics are things that all good companies want their employees to have.

Chapter 11

Persistence, Persistence, Persistence

Chapter 11: Persistence, Persistence, Persistence

You've picked the right job to apply for, crafted a fantastic resume, drafted a great cover letter email, studied for the interview, knocked it out of the park, and you've done everything that you need to do in order to properly follow up on the interview. The job is yours, right?

Well, no. No matter how hard you try, you can't "make" the company that has the job that you want give it to you. The best that you can hope for is that you make it easy for them to give it to you if they so choose.

What that means, of course, is that you just might not get the job. There could be a million reasons why today you were not the winner. The president's favorite nephew could have been interviewing for the same job. It turns out that the interviewer really doesn't like tall / short people. The perfect candidate who had actually done this very same job for a competitor came along after your interview.

When people are trying to sell a house that they own, they can become depressed if a lot of people are not showing up to take a look at it. A good realtor will remind them (over and over again) that all it takes to sell their house is one person who is willing to buy it.

You can only work at one professional job at a time. That means that you only need to find one company that is willing to offer you a job. The first company that you interview with for a job may not be that company. In fact, the first 10 companies that you interview with may not be that company. However, the good news is that the right company is out there and they are patient.

They are willing to wait for you. You need to be patient and willing to wait until you find and interview with them. Treat every interview that you participate in that does not result in a job offer that you want as exactly what it is: practice.

I almost hate to bring it up, but this is the perfect spot to remind you about what Thomas Edison said when he was asked about how he invented the light bulb. Although he tried thousands of times to create a working light bulb that didn't work his response was : "*I have not failed. I've just found 10,000 ways that won't work.*" The same (with hopefully smaller numbers) can be said about your job search: you will need to do some interview experiments before you find and get the perfect job.

I can assure you that if you apply everything that we've discussed in this book and you keep applying it and refining how you apply it, then you will eventually get the job that you are looking for. However, the one thing that I can't tell you is probably the one thing that you most want to know: how long is it going to take?

There is one other thing that I can promise you. If you give up, then you'll never get the job. Persistence is something that people both notice and value. Be very careful here: there is a big difference between being persistent and being annoying.

Being persistent means that you don't give up. You never stop trying to get the job until you've been told that it has been given to someone else. Being annoying means that you never leave people alone and you constantly badger them for more information on their decision.

You need to keep in mind that in most cases the people who will be making the hiring decision don't do this kind of job every day. What that means is that they've got a lot of other things on their plate and although getting the job might be the most important thing in your world, picking the right candidate is not the biggest thing in their world.

That's why being persistent and using the follow-up techniques that we've discussed is so valuable. You'll be able to stay on the edge of their awareness. This means that when they finally free up enough to wrap up the process of filling the position, they'll remember you (in a positive way) above everyone else.

Persistence, persistence, persistence. Just keep at it and eventually the perfect job that you are on the hunt for will be yours.

Chapter 12

The View From The Other Side: What Employers Are Looking For

Chapter 12:
The View From The Other Side: What Employers Are Looking For

As nerve-racking as the whole job hunt process is, from creating a resume to interviewing to following up, when I'm talking with students who are smack dab in the middle of the whole thing, the #1 question that they always ask me is "*What is this employer really looking for?*"

I feel your pain. If only you knew what they wanted, then you could spend your time making sure that you were giving it to them and not have to waste your time doing things that weren't necessary.

I've got some good news for you. I know the answer to this question. As somebody who has interviewed countless college students who were looking for their first professional job, I thought that I knew the answer. Just to be sure, I went out and talked to a number of different hiring managers who work in different fields than I do. It turns out that I only had some of the answers. The people that I talked with had all of the others.

When I was doing my interviews for this part of the book, I took page after page of notes. When I finally sat down to write the book I waded through those pages and made a discovery. All of the hiring managers that I had talked with had basically been asking for the same sorts of things. They may have used different words or expressed their wants in different terms, but in the end, they were all looking for the same things.

So that you don't have to, I've boiled it all down into the following pages of very valuable information. As you read this section realize that the words are coming from the people who will be sitting on the other side of the table from you. This is what they are really looking for from you.

Do You Have A Plan?

It seems rather basic doesn't it? However, the hiring managers that I talked with told me over and over again that they were amazed at the number of interview candidates that they talked to who really didn't have a clue as to what they really wanted to do with their lives.

The thinking goes that if you don't know what you want to accomplish in life, what it's going to take to make you happy, or even really why you went to college or chose the major that you did, then you won't be happy working for this company in this job.

However, on the flip side, if you know what your career goal is and you have a clear understanding of how this job is going to help you to make progress in getting there, then there's a very good chance that you'll do a good job in this position.

Persistence

Life is hard – sorry about that. One of the greatest fears that I hear expressed over and over again by the hiring managers that I talked with was that they were going to end up hiring one of those so-called "millennials" who had been raised by over protective parents and were used to having everything delivered to them on a platter and didn't know how to handle failure.

In every job, there are going to be challenges. Whoever gets hired for this job is going to have to have the skill set that will be needed in order to deal with the challenges and the setbacks that come along with the job.

This is the kind of thing that can't easily be taught. Instead, every employer is hoping that you already have the basic persistence skills that you are going to need in order to deal with everything that the job throws at you and find ways to still be successful.

Appearance

I don't care what your mom told you – looks count, especially during an interview. Hiring managers told me that how an interview candidate looks really contributes to the impression that they form about the person.

It's not just the clothes that you wear. It's everything: your hair, your fingernails, your handshake, your shoes, and how you present yourself. The hiring managers seemed to indicate that all of this contributed to answering one question: "*yes or no*".

Looking good won't necessarily get you the job. However, not looking good could end up costing you the job. Take the time to work on your appearance and at least this will be one less thing for you to have to worry about.

Enthusiasm

This one went by a number of different names: energy, attitude, excitement, etc. What the hiring managers were all talking about was a general sense of if you really wanted the job that you were interviewing for.

You need to keep in mind that the person that the company ends up hiring for this position is somebody that they are hoping will stay with the company for many years. That means that during the interview they need to make a decision as to if you would be someone that they would want to work with for a long time.

If you don't have enthusiasm, then what do you have? Basically you have negative energy. You are a downer to be around. Maybe you interviewed for the job because your parents told you that you had to. If you got the job, then sure, you'd probably do the work, but you wouldn't be happy about it. Nobody wants to work with somebody like that.

Communication Skills

This is a big one. In a traditional work environment, you will be one of many people who are all working together in order to make the company a success. The person who gets hired is being hired at least in part because the company believes that they will bring their great ideas to the table and will be able to help the company do more.

If you have great ideas, then they will do nobody any good if they stay trapped inside of your head. What this means is that you are going to have to be able to communicate your ideas to the people that you work with. How good are your communication skills?

Hiring managers told me that they are looking for candidates who can take multiple ideas and assemble them into a single clear vision. They then want that person to be able to communicate the vision to the smartest person at the company as well as the least smart person. Once again, this is a skill that they need the person that they select to be able to walk in the door with.

Be Humble

You are not interviewing for a job to run the company. You had better not show up for the interview with an attitude that says "*this company would be lucky to have me work for them*". If you do, they just may look for ways to get along without you…

Hiring managers told me that what they are looking for are candidates who understand that advancement within the company comes as a result of hard work. If you show that you realize that the position that you are interviewing for is just the start of a journey within the company, instead of the final job that you'll ever have there, then you've got the right mind set.

What the hiring managers were trying to determine during the interview was if you would do your best in the job that they were trying to fill. If your sights were set on positions higher up in the company, then maybe the current job would not get the attention and effort that it needed. Prove to the interviewer that this is the job that you want and the one that you'll work hard at and you'll have put this issue to bed.

Confidence

This is a tricky one – the line that separates being confident from being cocky is a very fine line indeed. Being confident is good, being cocky is not.

What the hiring managers told me that they were looking for were candidates who were self-confidant. This will come across in the interview if you can show the interviewer that you are comfortable with yourself. There is no one way to show this, but it will be the result of a whole bunch of little things. If you admit that you are not perfect, if you state that you look forward to having an opportunity to do things that you've not done before, and if you communicate that you believe that you've learned a lot while in school, all of these will go a long way towards communicating your confidence.

What they are desperately trying to avoid is hiring somebody who will start to make excuses as to why work is not getting done. They want to hire somebody who has a positive attitude and believes that they will be able to accomplish a task on time.

Pleasing Personality

This one is pretty simple – are you a person that the interviewer would actually want to spend time with. During the interview, did you come across as a person who has done interesting things and would be enjoyable to work with?

The one thing that the hiring managers wanted to avoid was selecting a candidate who had no personality. This is the kind of person who is there, but whom you quickly forget. They don't bring anything to a discussion and so they can't really contribute to solving problems. Nobody wants to work with them.

Resourcefulness

When you were in school, for many of the problems that you were asked to solve in your classes you could just turn to the back of the book and the answers to at least the odd numbered problems would be there. Real life doesn't work that way.

Instead, when the person who gets hired for the position that you are interviewing for comes face-to-face with a problem, they are going to have to create their own solutions. This is where your resourcefulness is going to have to come into play.

It can be hard to get a handle on this during the short time that is available during an interview. However, the hiring managers that I talked to said that if the candidate seems to know a great deal about the company and the industry then it shows that they've taken the initiative to find out. This leads the interviewer to believe that they have the resourcefulness that will be needed to do well in the job that they are interviewing for.

Initiative

Sadly, national "*bring your Mom to work day*" never got off the ground so when the company hires somebody to fill this open position, only that person will be showing up. What this means is that whom they select is going to have to show that they can take the initiative and do the work.

Jobs don't come with operating instructions. What that means is that the person that the company hires for this position is going to have to be self-motivated and go out there and find out what they have to do. The ones who take the initiative to do this and who are goal setters are the ones who will be successful.

If you can show during the interview that you've taken the initiative in the past, then you'll leave the interviewer with the impression that you'll move up the so-called corporate ladder quickly and that's the kind of person that the company wants to hire.

Responsibility

Responsibility is a big word that we often hear our parents use ("*You need to learn to be more responsible...*") but we don't spend a lot of time thinking about what it actually means. It turns out that we should.

Hiring managers are looking for candidates who will be able to take on responsibility as a part of their job. What this means is that they can be told what to do, and then they'll actually go off and do it.

If you can show that you've accepted responsibility as a part of your previous activities perhaps as a part of student government, a club officer, community involvement, or even as the leader of a sports team, then this will go a long way towards showing that you can handle responsibility. This is the kind of person that the interviewer is looking to have join their company.

The Ability To Work In Teams

A reality of the real world of work is that we don't work alone. The size of the team that you'll be a part of can range from two to hundreds, but the key is that in order to be valuable to the company, you are going to have to be able to play well with others.

Hiring managers can all think of horror stories in their past when they've brought someone onto their team who didn't want to work with the other people who were already on the team. These "hidden loners" end up causing a great deal of trouble not only for the team, but also for the hiring manager. They desperately don't want to repeat that mistake.

This means that they are going to be looking for examples of when you accomplished a task as a member of a team. You'll probably be asked pointed questions about how that went: did you get along with the other people on the team, did you enjoy it, and do you prefer to work by yourself? Keep in mind that they are trying to determine if adding you to their team will help or hurt the team.

A Sense Of Ethics

Of all of the things that the hiring manager needs to determine during an interview, this can be the most difficult. Pick up almost any paper these days and there will be another story about an employee being lead off to jail because they made the wrong ethical decision.

Your sense of ethical values is something that you probably don't display in normal conversations. The hiring manager is going to have to tease it out of you. This may be done by off-hand things that he or she brings up in casual conversations before, during or after the formal interview. It may also come up as specific questions during the interview.

The simplest advice that I can give you here after having taught a college-level ethics course is that the right answer to any ethics question is to always choose the hard or difficult thing to do. The easy path or the one that provides the most immediate value to you is almost always the wrong decision to make!

Conclusion

Now you know everything that I know about how to find your first job when you get out of college. In the end, it turns out that it's really a pretty simple, straightforward process.

The biggest challenge that most college students have when they start their first job search is that it seems to have no end to it. You can do all of the right things: pick a job, create a resume and a cover letter, interview, and follow up and still end up not getting the job. It turns out that that's ok.

A job hunt is a process. I can't tell you how long it is going to take you to find the perfect job for you. However, I can tell you that it's all going to be worth it. Finding and getting the right job is what is going to make those long years of attending college all worthwhile.

You've already done the hard work: you have (or you will) earned a college degree. Finding a job is much simpler than everything that you have already accomplished. Since you've read this book, you now know all of the secrets that you'll need in order to be successful.

Now go out there and find your perfect job!

Appendix A:

Goals For Your Job Search

In order to accomplish a successful job search, you need to break this big problem up into a set of smaller more easily attained goals. As you achieve each goal, you'll realize that you are now one step closer to getting the perfect job for you. This will provide you with the motivation and the drive to continue your quest.

Your specific set of job hunt goals will be yours and yours alone. Just to help you get started, here is a sample list of goals in proper sequential order that a number of college students have used in the past to guide their job hunt. Feel free to use them as a starting point for your hunt:

1. Answer the 3 critical questions listed in Chapter 1
2. Create a plan for you to get work experience in an area that you'd like to get a job in.
3. Create a LinkedIn account
4. Load personal contact information and a photo into your LinkedIn account.
5. Join LinkedIn groups that relate to work areas that you are interested in. Read group postings once a day.
6. Build your work experience in LinkedIn
7. Create a resume
8. Create a sample cover letter
9. Sign up for your first on-campus job interview
10. Attend your first on-campus job interview

11. Do a written self-evaluation after the interview to identify what you should do differently next time. Document what questions they asked and what your answers were. Create better answers.
12. Follow up with the interviewer after the interview in order to try out your follow up skills.
13. Review job postings associated with your LinkedIn groups
14. Use your university professors to jump-start your LinkedIn network.
15. Maximize the benefit of on campus interviews by signing up for as many as possible. Find something that you like about each position and focus on that.
16. Evaluate yourself after each interview – what can you do better next time.

Appendix B:

What You Need To Learn From Every College Job

Gaining work experience while you are in college is a great way to make yourself appear more attractive to prospective employers once you graduate. What too many college students don't realize is that every job can teach you two things: what you enjoy doing and what you don't enjoy doing. Use the following form to capture what you've learned when your next job wraps up and then use this information when you start your job search:

What I Enjoyed Doing As A Part Of This Job:

1.
2.
3.
4.
5.

Things that I Really Didn't Like To Do That Were Part Of This Job:

1.
2.
3.
4.
5.

What one thing do you now know about what your perfect job will look like that you didn't know before you had this job?

Appendix C:

What To Do AFTER You Get The Perfect Job

What too many college students don't realize is that once they've accepted that perfect job offer, their job hunt is not done. To get to where they are, a lot of people had to lend them a helping hand and it's now time to update them.

When people provide you with guidance, suggestion, or perhaps even make contacts to help you with your job search, they have become part of the process. What this means is that they want to know how the story turns out.

During your job hunt, there will probably be many people who lent you assistance. You need to be sure to keep careful notes on who did what to help you. This is going to be important later on.

Once you've got the job, you now need to reach out and update everyone who helped you. You've got to let them know that you got the job! This is important for couple of different reasons.

The first is that you may need their help again sometime in the future. Reaching back and letting them know that their help was appreciated means that they will be more likely to help you out again in the future. Additionally, you want them to feel good about having helped you in the past – they want to know that their help was valuable to you. If the advice or contacts that they provided you with didn't help, then they will want to know that so that they can be of more help to the next person.

Remember – getting the job is not the last step. Make sure that you take the time to update and thank all of the people who made getting that job possible. By doing this, you'll be once again preparing for the future.

Appendix D:

100 Common Interview Questions

Basic Questions:

1. Tell me about yourself.
2. What are your strengths?
3. What are your weaknesses?
4. Why do you want this job?
5. Where would you like to be in your career five years from now?
6. What's your ideal company?
7. What attracted you to this company?
8. Why should we hire you?
9. What did you like least about your last job?
10. When were you most satisfied in your job?
11. What can you do for us that other candidates can't?
12. What were the responsibilities of your last position?
13. Why are you leaving your present job?
14. What do you know about this industry?
15. What do you know about our company?
16. Are you willing to relocate?
17. Do you have any questions for me?

Behavioral Questions:

18. What was the last project you headed up, and what was its outcome?
19. Give me an example of a time that you felt you went above and beyond the call of duty at work.
20. Can you describe a time when your work was criticized?
21. Have you ever been on a team where someone was not pulling their own weight? How did you handle it?

22. Tell me about a time when you had to give someone difficult feedback. How did you handle it?
23. What is your greatest failure, and what did you learn from it?
24. What irritates you about other people, and how do you deal with it?
25. If I were your supervisor and asked you to do something that you disagreed with, what would you do?
26. What was the most difficult period in your life, and how did you deal with it?
27. Give me an example of a time you did something wrong. How did you handle it?
28. What irritates you about other people, and how do you deal with it?
29. Tell me about a time where you had to deal with conflict on the job.
30. If you were at a business lunch and you ordered a rare steak and they brought it to you well done, what would you do?
31. If you found out your company was doing something against the law, like fraud, what would you do?
32. What assignment was too difficult for you, and how did you resolve the issue?
33. What's the most difficult decision you've made in the last two years and how did you come to that decision?
34. Describe how you would handle a situation if you were required to finish multiple tasks by the end of the day, and there was no conceivable way that you could finish them.

Tell Me More About You:

35. How would you describe your work style?
36. What would be your ideal working environment?
37. What do you look for in terms of culture -- structured or entrepreneurial?
38. Give examples of ideas you've had or implemented.
39. What techniques and tools do you use to keep yourself organized?
40. If you had to choose one, would you consider yourself a big-picture person or a detail-oriented person?
41. Tell me about your proudest achievement.
42. Who was your favorite manager and why?
43. What do you think of your previous boss?
44. Was there a person in your career who really made a difference?
45. What kind of personality do you work best with and why?
46. What are you most proud of?
47. What do you like to do?
48. What are your lifelong dreams?
49. What do you ultimately want to become?
50. What is your personal mission statement?
51. What are three positive things your last boss would say about you?
52. What negative thing would your last boss say about you?
53. What three character traits would your friends use to describe you?
54. What are three positive character traits you don't have?

55. If you were interviewing someone for this position, what traits would you look for?
56. List five words that describe your character.
57. Who has impacted you most in your career and how?
58. What is your greatest fear?
59. What is your biggest regret and why?
60. What's the most important thing you learned in school?
61. Why did you choose your major?
62. What will you miss about your present/last job?
63. What is your greatest achievement outside of work?
64. What are the qualities of a good leader? A bad leader?
65. Do you think a leader should be feared or liked?
66. How do you feel about taking no for an answer?
67. How would you feel about working for someone who knows less than you?
68. How do you think I rate as an interviewer?
69. Tell me one thing about yourself you wouldn't want me to know.
70. Tell me the difference between good and exceptional.
71. What kind of car do you drive?
72. There's no right or wrong answer, but if you could be anywhere in the world right now, where would you be?
73. What's the last book you read?
74. What magazines do you subscribe to?
75. What's the best movie you've seen in the last year?
76. What would you do if you won the lottery?

77. Who are your heroes?
78. What do you like to do for fun?
79. What do you do in your spare time?
80. What is your favorite memory from childhood?

Your Career Questions:

81. What are you looking for in terms of career development?
82. How do you want to improve yourself in the next year?
83. What kind of goals would you have in mind if you got this job?
84. If I were to ask your last supervisor to provide you additional training or exposure, what would she suggest?

How Would You Get Started Questions:

85. How would you go about establishing your credibility quickly with the team?
86. How long will it take for you to make a significant contribution?
87. What do you see yourself doing within the first 30 days of this job?
88. If selected for this position, can you describe your strategy for the first 90 days?

Your Salary Questions:

89. What salary are you seeking?
90. What's your salary history?

91. If I were to give you this salary you requested but let you write your job description for the next year, what would it say?

Outside Of The Box Questions

92. How many times do a clock's hands overlap in a day?
93. How would you weigh a plane without scales?
94. Tell me 10 ways to use a pencil other than writing.
95. Sell me this pencil.
96. If you were an animal, which one would you want to be?
97. Why is there fuzz on a tennis ball?
98. If you could choose one superhero power, what would it be and why?
99. If you could get rid of any one of the US states, which one would you get rid of and why?
100. With your eyes closed, tell me step-by-step how to tie my shoes.

Appendix E:

Good Questions For You To Ask During An Interview

More often than not during an interview, towards the end of the interview, the interviewer will turn to you and ask you if you have any questions that you'd like to ask them. This is your moment to shine!

One of the things that you need to keep in mind is that when the interview is over, the last thing that you talked about with them is what is going to be in their minds. That means that you want to wrap things up on a high note. Here is a list of sample questions that you can use as a starting point for crafting your own very good set of questions to ask your interviewer:

1. In this position, what would my duties / responsibilities be?

2. To whom would I report? What can you tell me about their background?

3. Would I be reporting to multiple people? What is their role in the company?

4. Every job experiences a great deal of change over time. Does the company provide any form of on-going training for its employees?

5. Can you tell me anything about what types of equipment I would be required to use in this job?

6. Does the company have an annual performance review for each employee and how does that work?

7. What future positions have people who have held this job moved on to?

8. What do you feel are this company's special strengths?

9. Can you tell me how long you have been with the company? Where did you work before you joined the company?

10. What do you like the most about your job?

11. Can you tell me what the company's goals for the next year are?

12. Who are your most successful employees and how did they do it?

13. What characteristics have you noticed in the company's employees who have done especially well here?

14. Can you tell me what type of person you are looking for in order to fill this position?

Hard work does not
guarantee success;
However, success does
not happen
without hard work.

– Dr. Jim Anderson

 The world's largest professional association for the advancement of technology

No matter what your major is, becoming a student member of the IEEE is a great Idea.

Look at what membership gets you:
- Exclusive benefits for students
- Knowledge
- Community
- Profession
- Additional memberships
- IEEE Member Discounts
- Additional products

Free Microsoft software!
- Expression Studio 4 Ultimate
- Expression Web Designer
- Project Professional 2010
- Visio Professional 2010
- Visual Studio 2010 Ultimate
- Vista Business Edition
- Windows Vista Enterprise
- Windows XP Professional

One software license per student membership is allowed each year of active IEEE student or graduate student membership. License terms also require that software use is for educational and research purposes only.

Join the IEEE by visiting: http://www.ieee.org

America's Top Student Career Speaker!

Dr. Jim Anderson is available to present his speeches to college student audiences nationwide.

Dr. Anderson believes that in order to both learn and remember what he says, students need to laugh. Each one of his speeches is full of fun and humor so that what he says "sticks" with everyone.

Dr. Anderson's Speech Topics:

- **How To Find The Right 1st Job Using LinkedIn**
    - How to find companies who have the jobs that you'll want.
- **10 Secrets For Having A Great Career**
    - How to get recognized for the work that you do.
- **How To Create & Give Fantastic Presentations**
    - How to connect the opening to the closing
- **Ethics Are Sooo Boring... Until You're Going To Jail!**
    - How to recognize an ethical problem.

Dr. Jim Anderson presents over 100 speeches per year. To invite Dr. Anderson to speak at your event, contact him at:

Phone: 813-418-6970 or
Email: *jim@BlueElephantConsulting.com*

Photo Credits:

Cover - By: dospaz,
http://www.flickr.com/photos/59195512@N00/4423741740/in/photostream/

Chapter 1 - By: mac_filko
http://www.flickr.com/photos/mac_filko/5486368637/

Chapter 2 - By: mconnors
http://www.morguefile.com/archive/display/2190

Chapter 3 - By: cohdra
http://www.morguefile.com/archive/display/83361

Chapter 4 – By: toddalert
http://www.flickr.com/photos/toddler/3450871850/

Chapter 5 – By: mariosundar
http://www.flickr.com/photos/mariosundar/470973290/

Chaoter 6 – By: Nguyen Vu Hung
http://www.flickr.com/photos/vuhung/7158921905/

Chapter 7 – By: dbbent
http://www.flickr.com/photos/zengei/6943077858/

Chapter 8 – By: sideshowmom
http://www.morguefile.com/archive/display/93790

Chapter 9 – By: stevendepolo
http://www.flickr.com/photos/stevendepolo/6228420376/

Chapter 10 – By: asenat29
http://www.flickr.com/photos/72153088@N08/6510934443/

Chapter 11 – By: Lyndi&Jason
http://www.flickr.com/photos/citnaj/1362274601/

Chapter 12 – By: gerlos
http://www.flickr.com/photos/gerlos/3119891607/

Appendix A – By: Stefano Moscardini
http://www.flickr.com/photos/mosca27/166707333/

Appendix B – By: xololounge
http://www.morguefile.com/archive/display/227431

Appendix C: -- By: Emily Jones
http://www.flickr.com/photos/emilywaltonjones/1111795739/

Appendix D – By: Colin Kinner
http://www.flickr.com/photos/colinkinner/2200500024/

Appendix E – By: Cesar Bojorquez
http://www.flickr.com/photos/uncut/16926192/

www.ingramcontent.com/pod-product-compliance
Lightning Source LLC
Chambersburg PA
CBHW061508180526
45171CB00001B/86